Honey, If It Wasn't for You

Barron Ryan

Illustrated by
Cali Ward

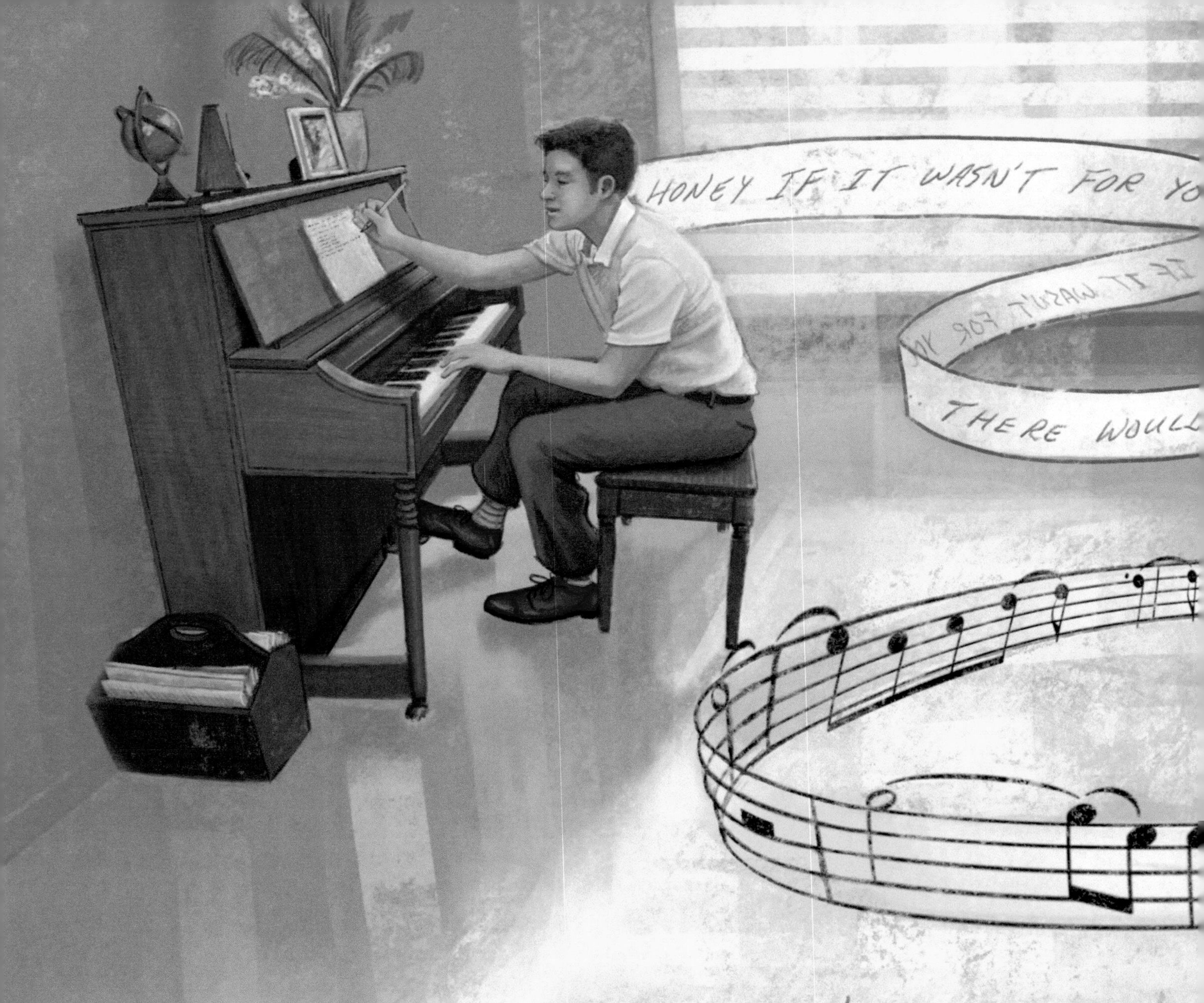
HONEY IF IT WASN'T FOR
THERE

This is the true story of a song by Don Feagin and me. He wrote the words and I wrote the music. But this wasn't your average partnership.

That's because Don died in 1981—six years before I was even born.

Honey, If It Wasn't for You

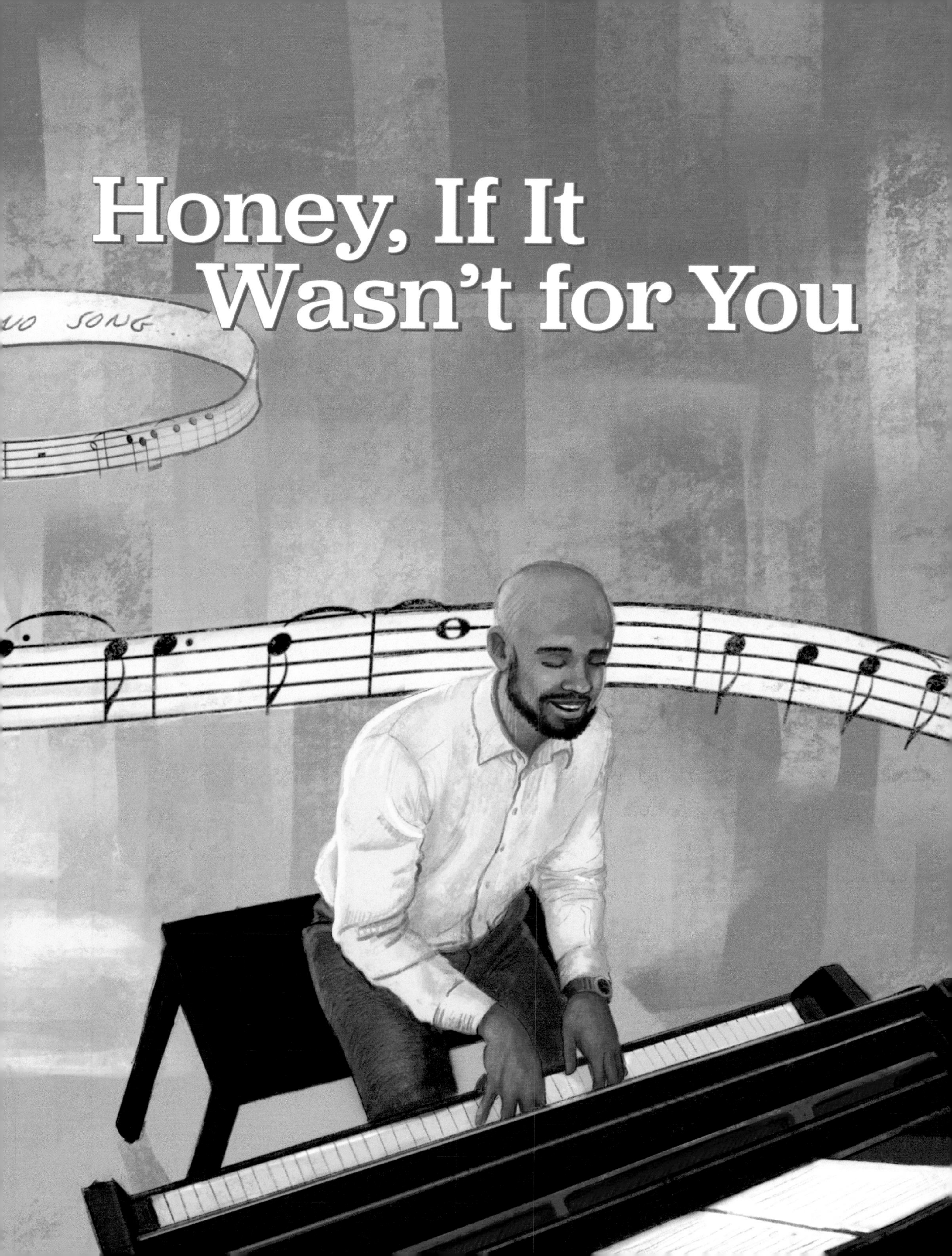

To the outside world, Don Feagin seemed ordinary enough. He had a wife he loved, a beautiful home, and a passion for music.

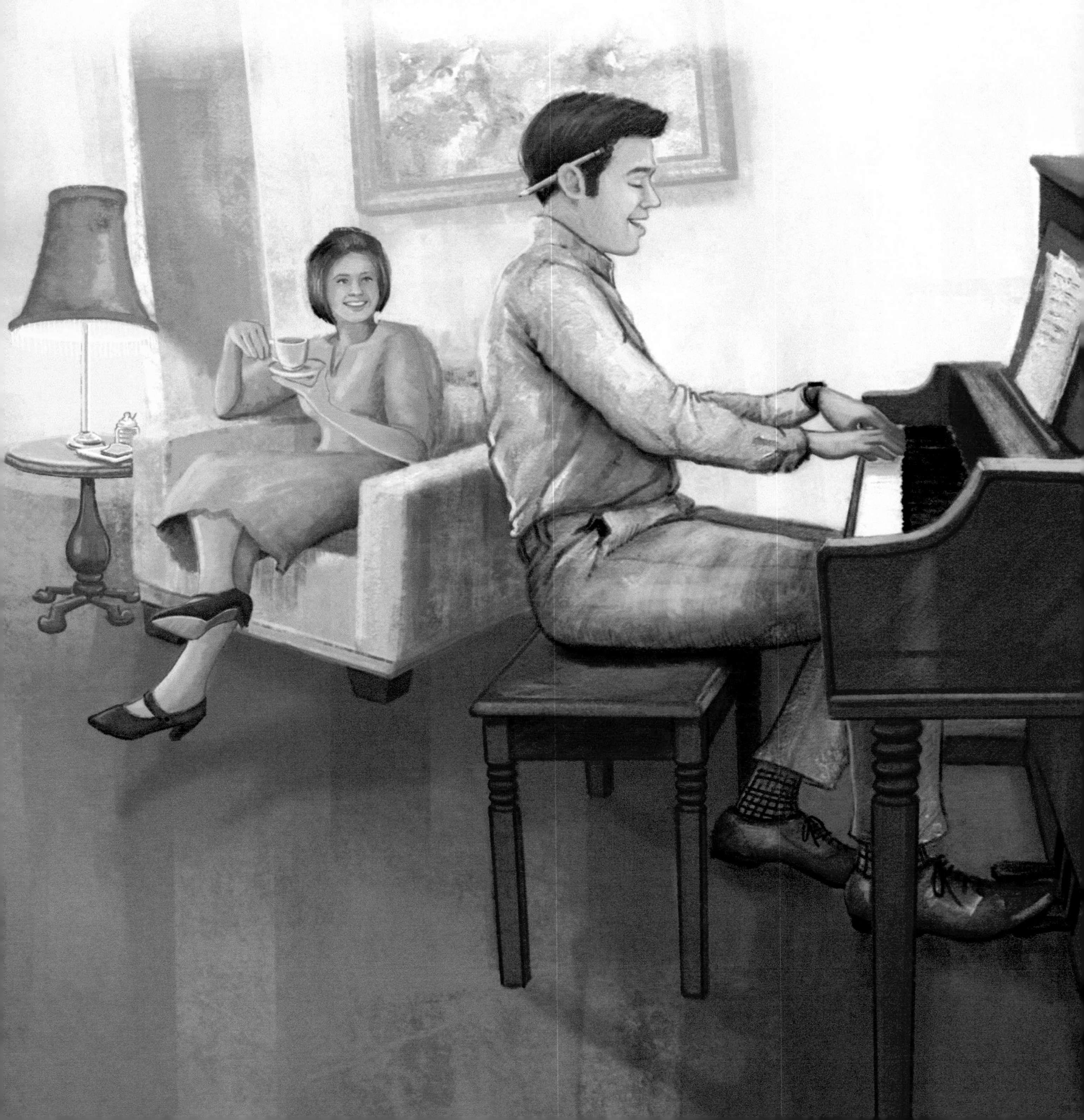

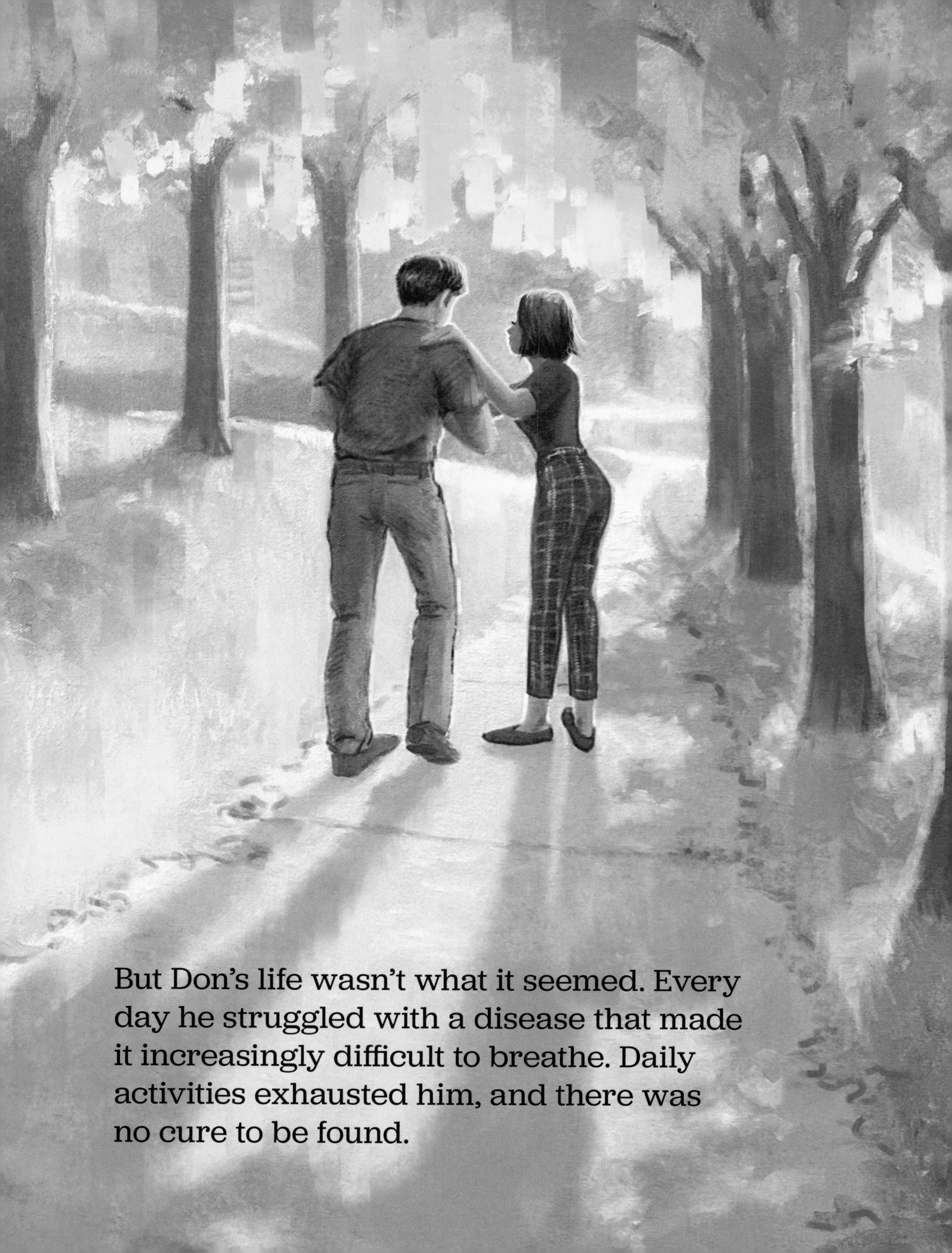

But Don's life wasn't what it seemed. Every day he struggled with a disease that made it increasingly difficult to breathe. Daily activities exhausted him, and there was no cure to be found.

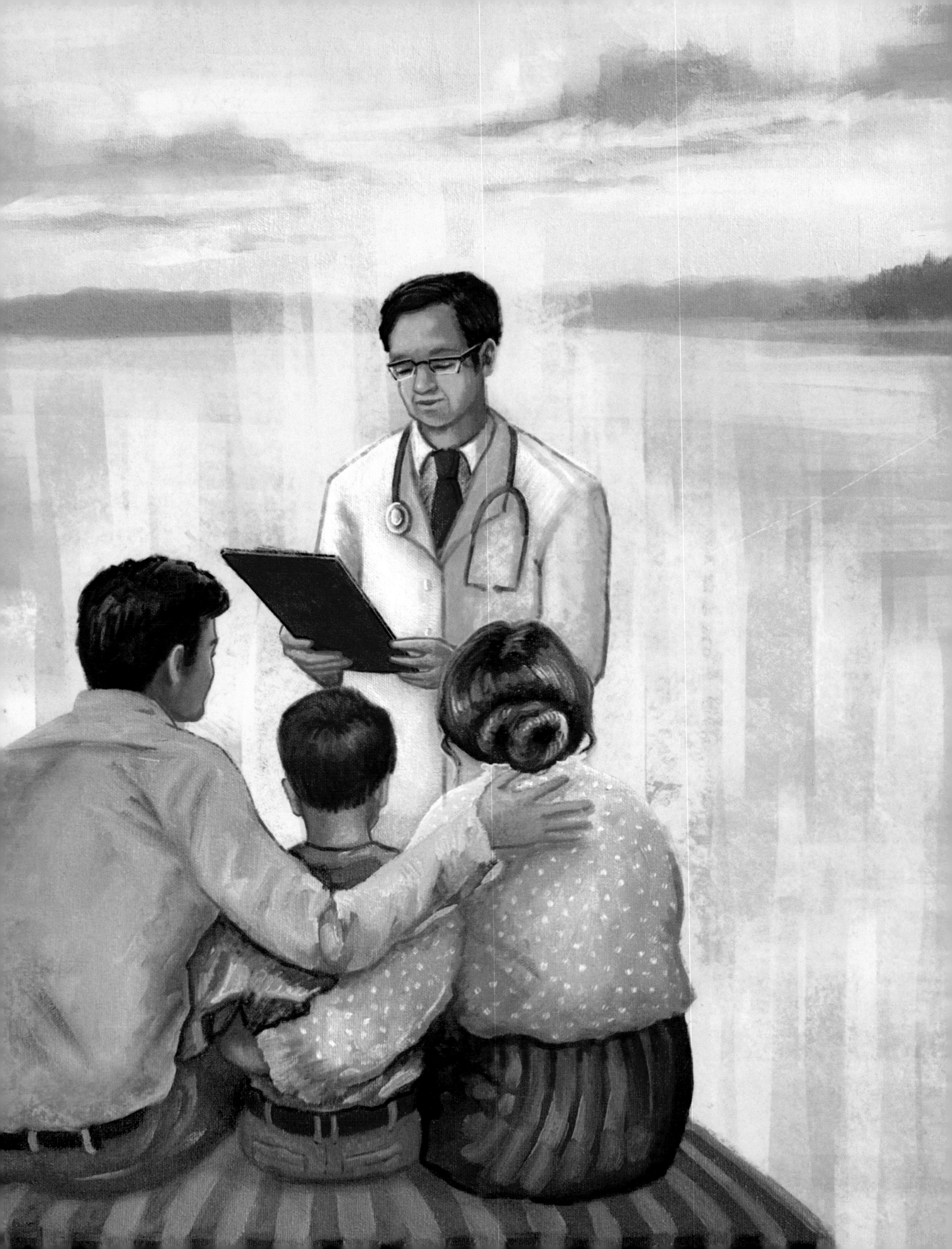

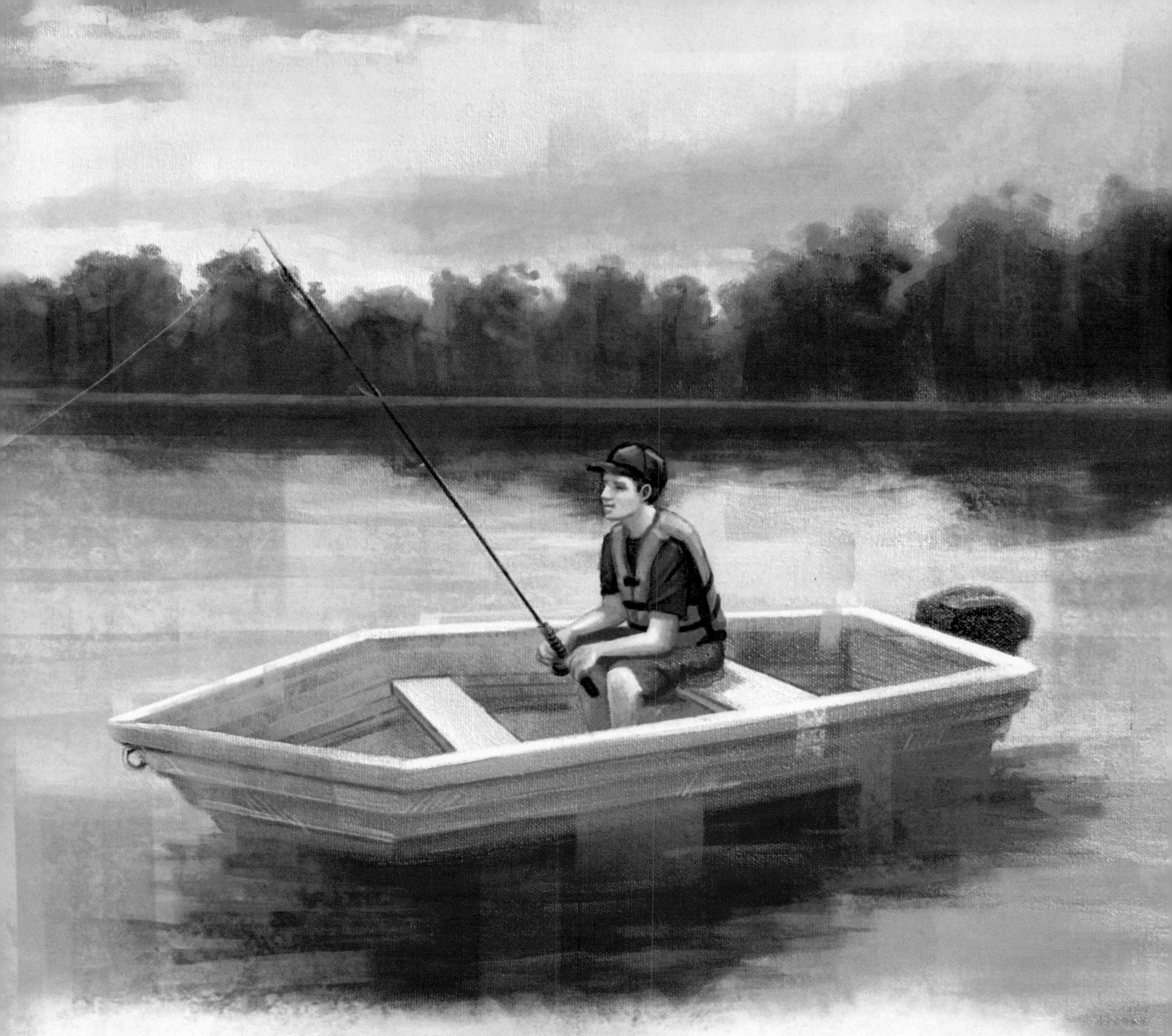

Don had known from the time he was young that he wouldn't live as long as most. He had, in fact, already exceeded expectations simply by surviving to adulthood.

Still, Don was determined to live a full life.

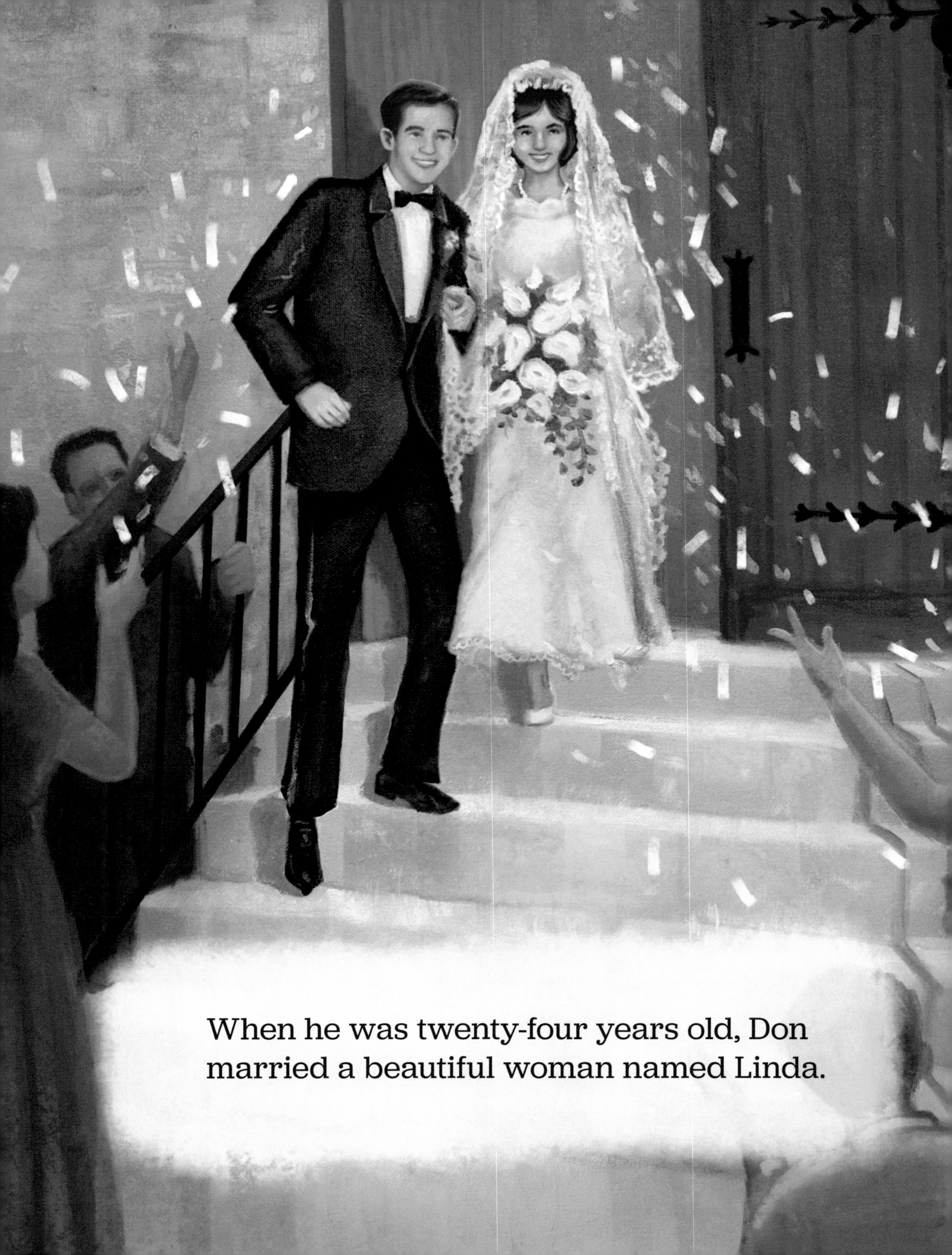

When he was twenty-four years old, Don married a beautiful woman named Linda.

They knew their marriage would be difficult, but resolved that their love was worth the burdens they would bear.

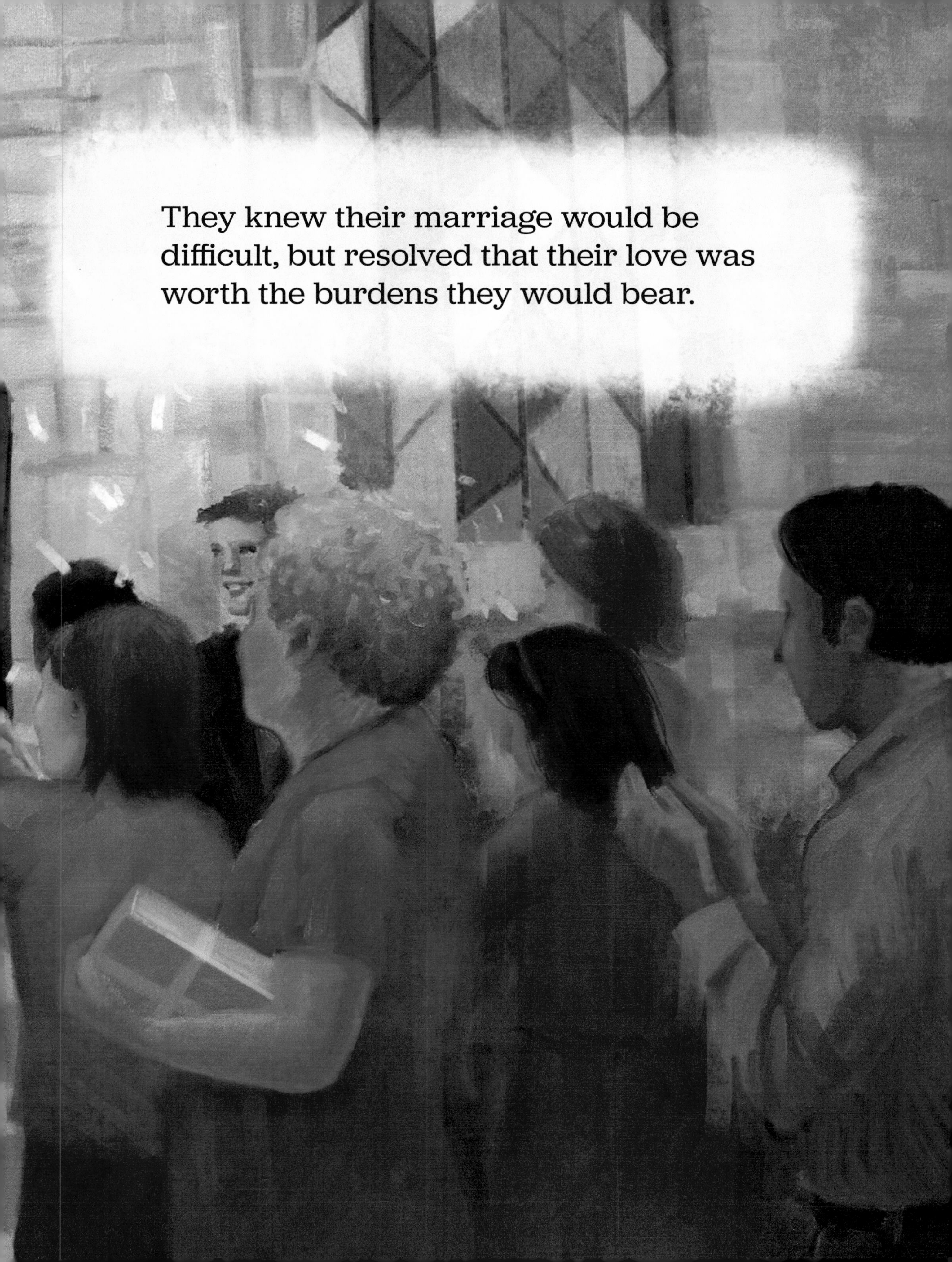

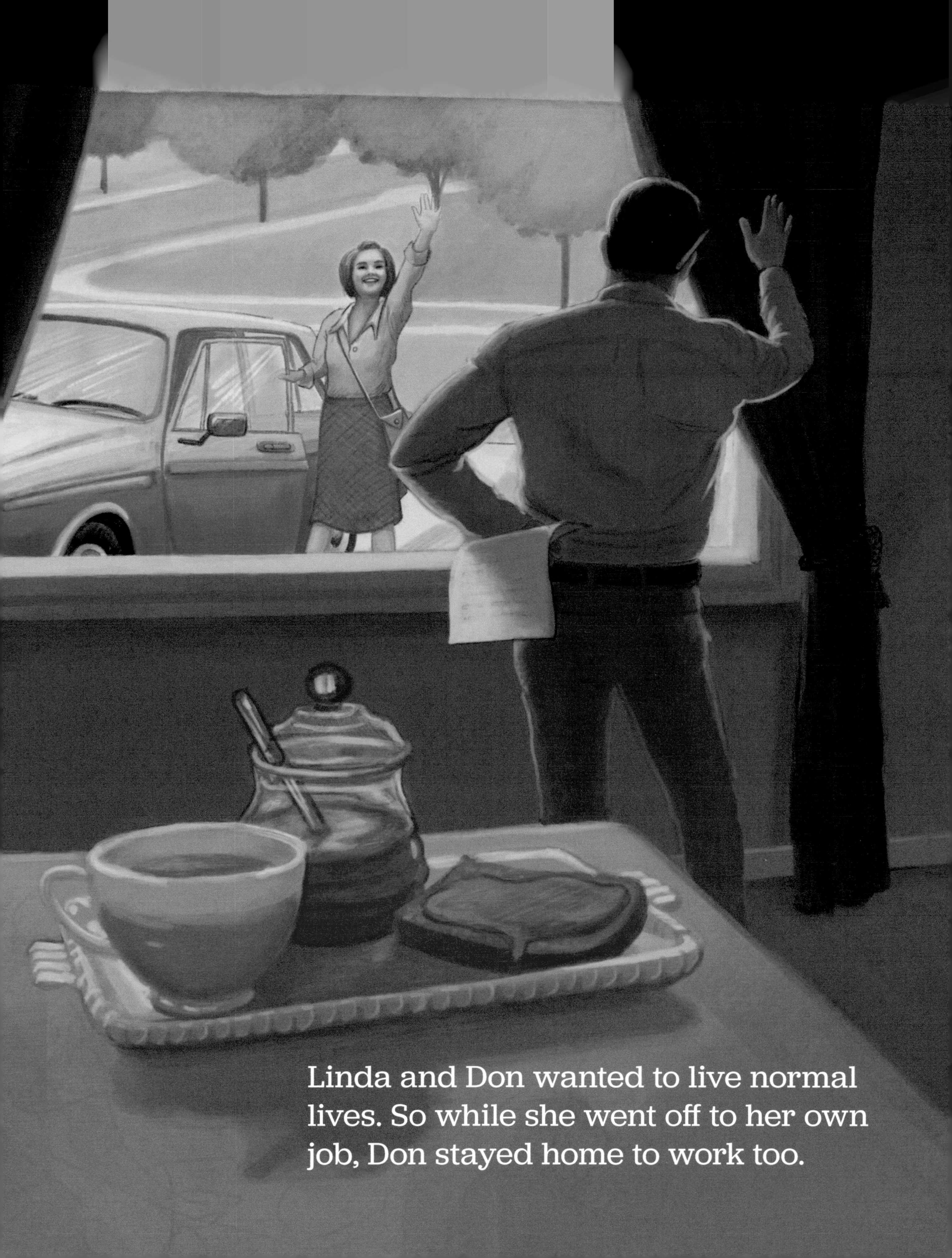

Linda and Don wanted to live normal lives. So while she went off to her own job, Don stayed home to work too.

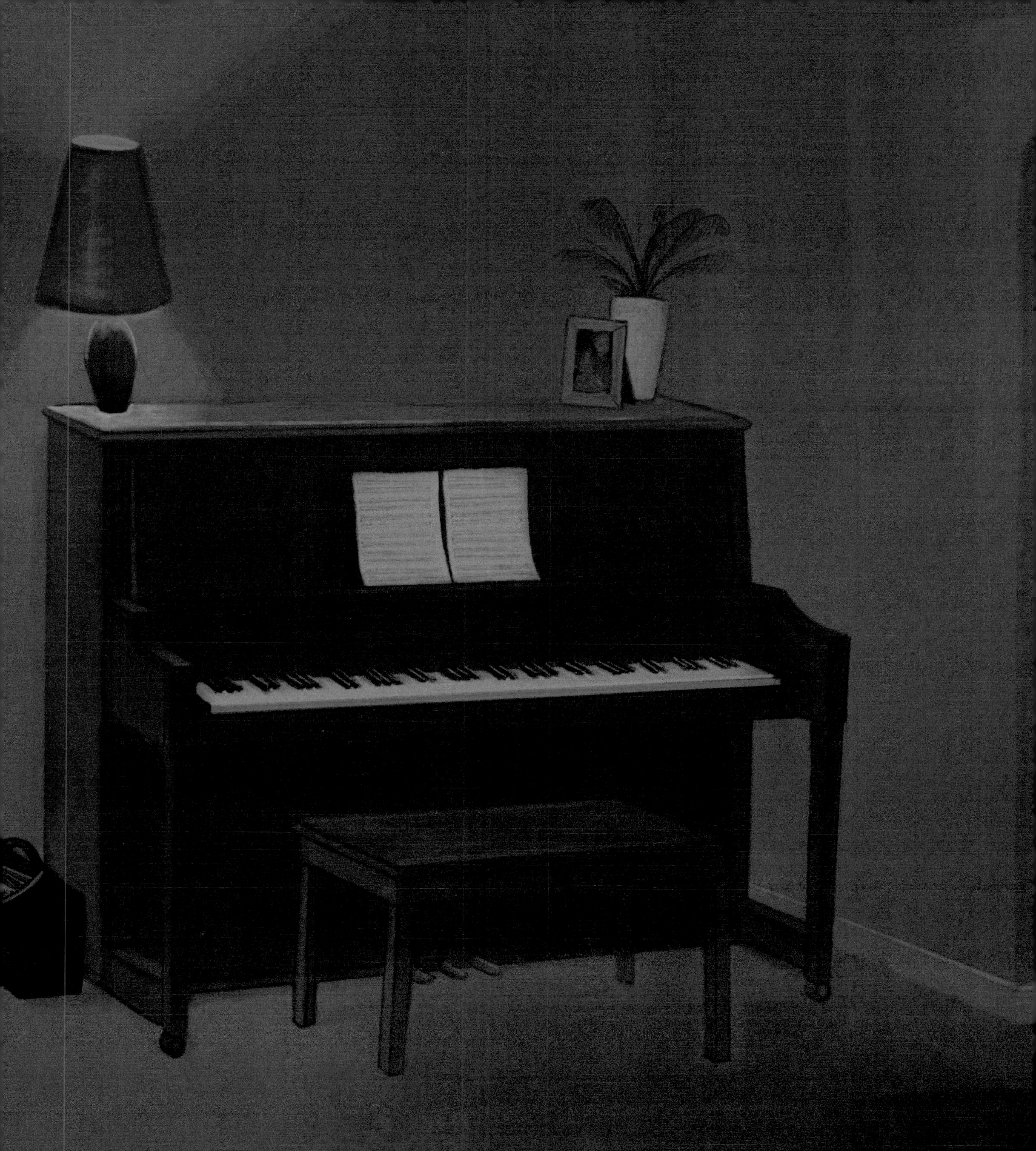

His job was composing songs for famous musicians to record. But he also had ideas of his own. In his spare time, Don wrote songs just for himself.

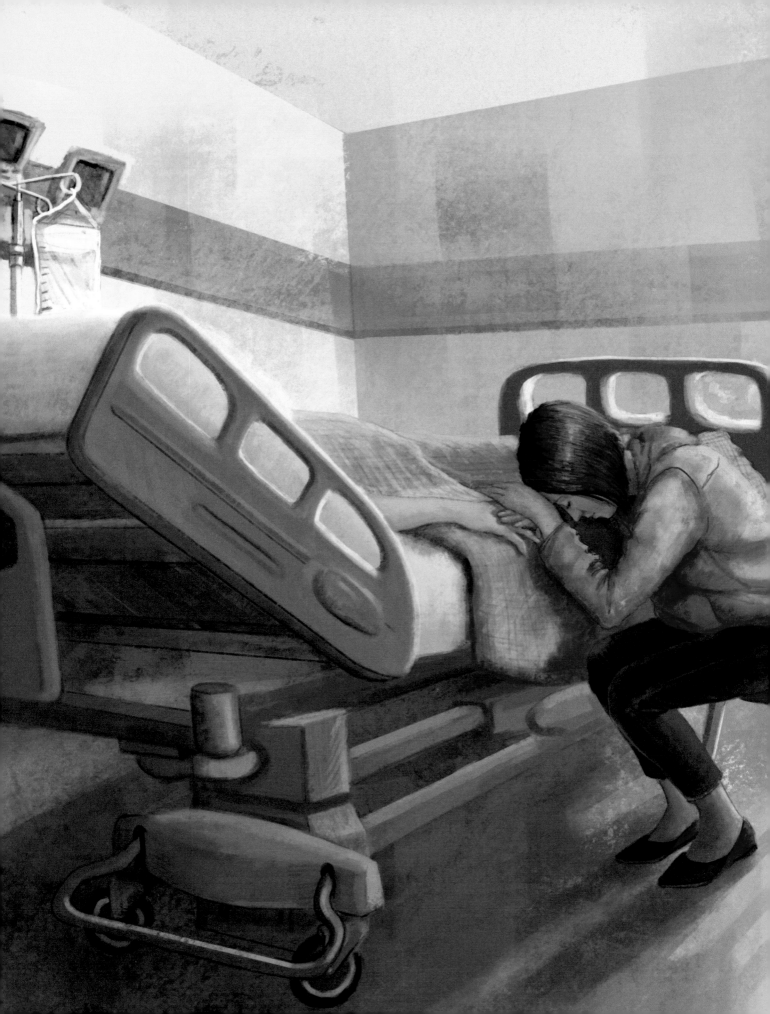

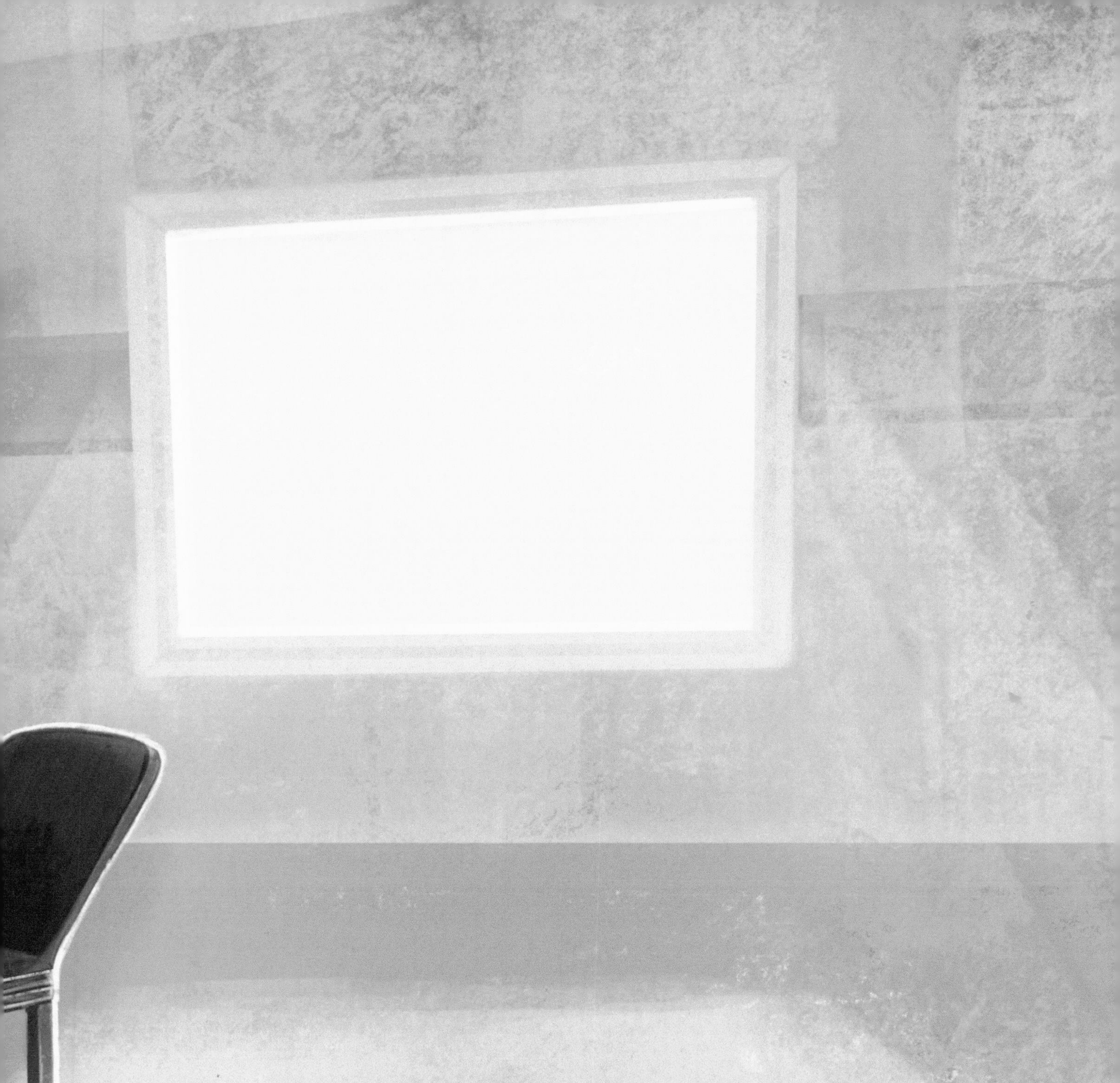

As time wore on, living with Don's
disease became more challenging.

Then in 1981, at age thirty-eight,
Don passed away.

Linda was heartbroken. Going through his belongings, she found boxes of his song lyrics.

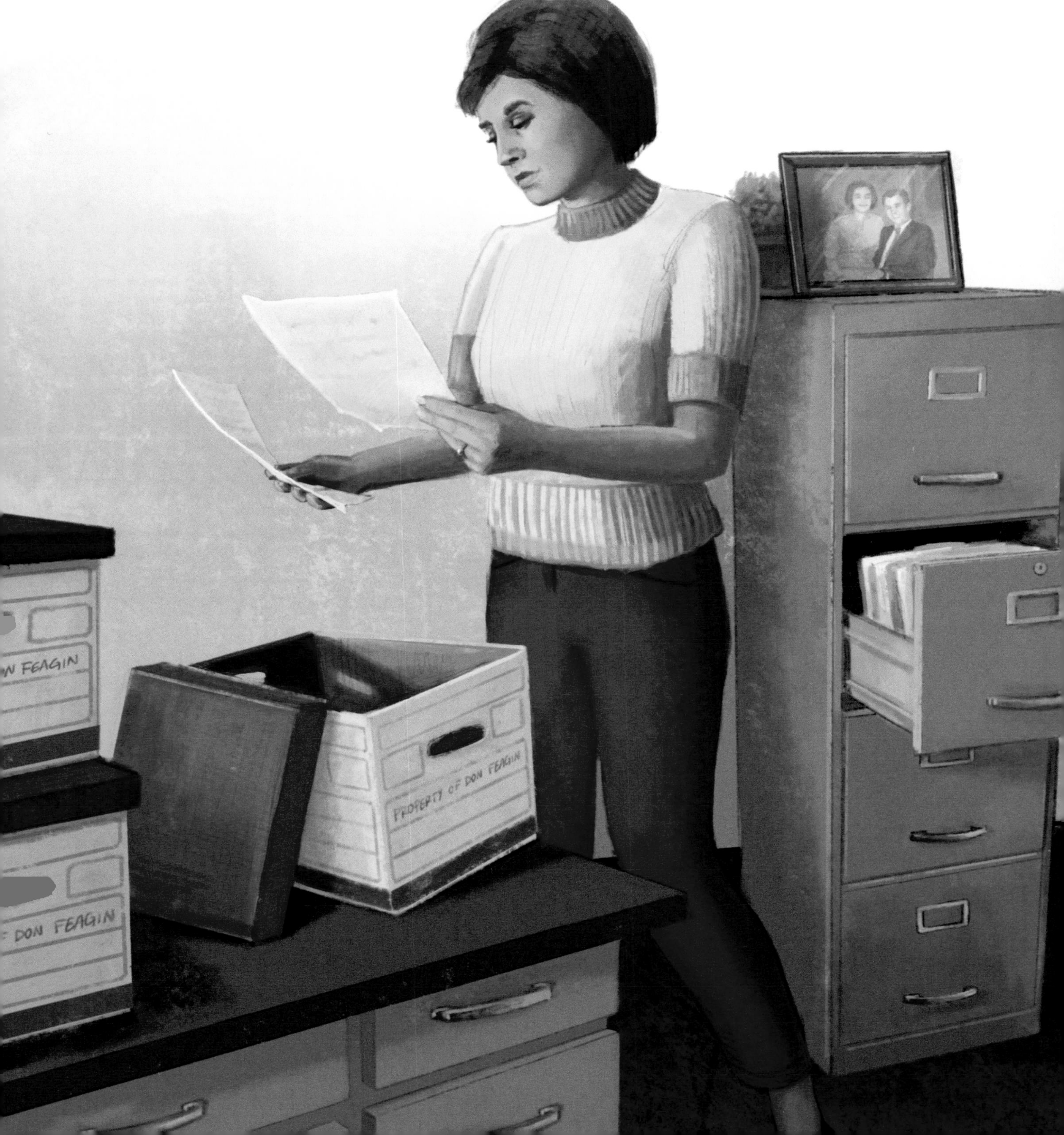
PROPERTY OF DON FEAGIN
DON FEAGIN

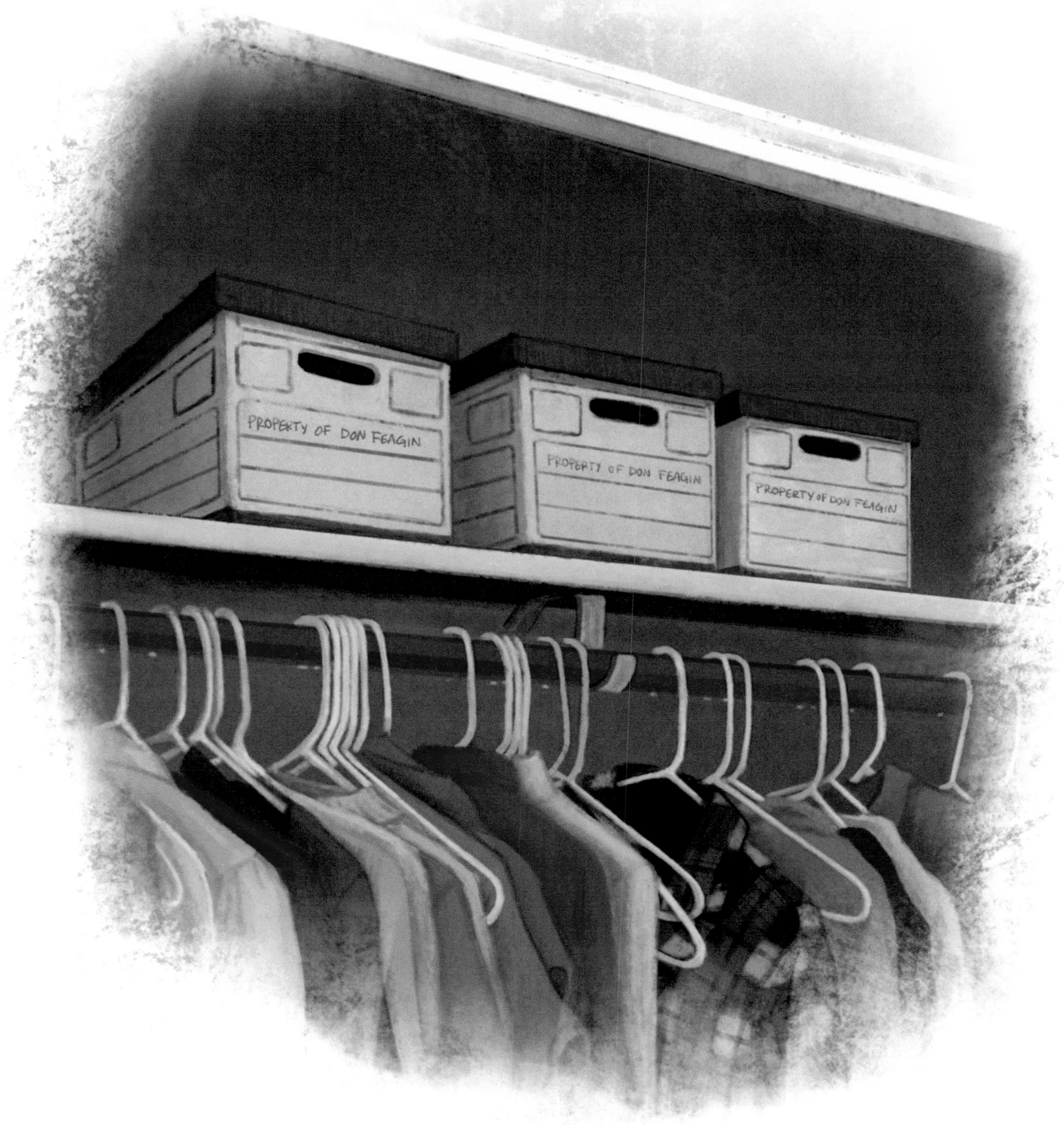
PROPERTY OF DON FEAGIN
PROPERTY OF DON FEAGIN
PROPERTY OF DON FEAGIN

The thought of opening the boxes was too much for her. So she put them out of sight, where she wouldn't have to think about them.

For decades, those boxes sat untouched.

And they might have stayed that way, if not for a fateful visit to a concert many years later.

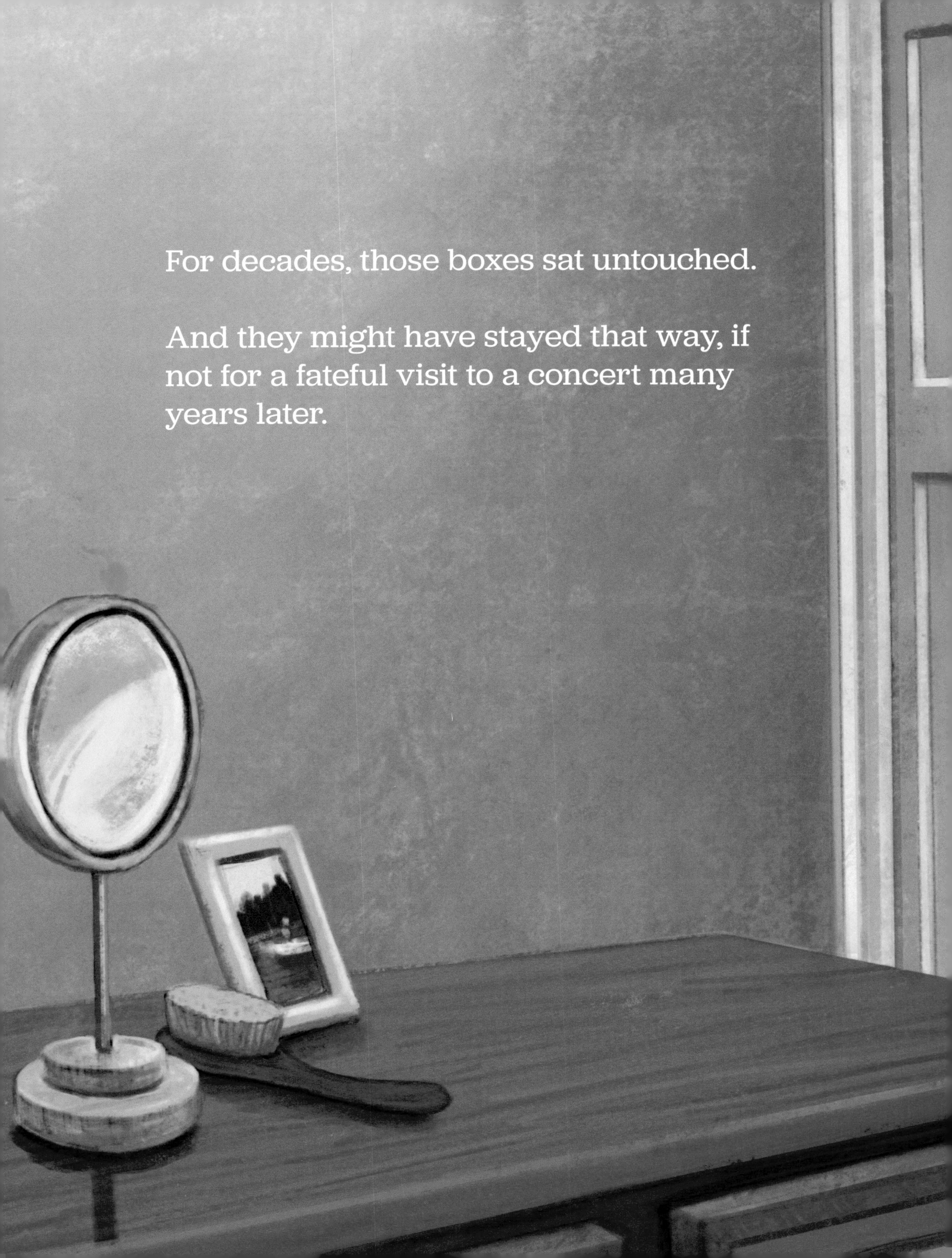

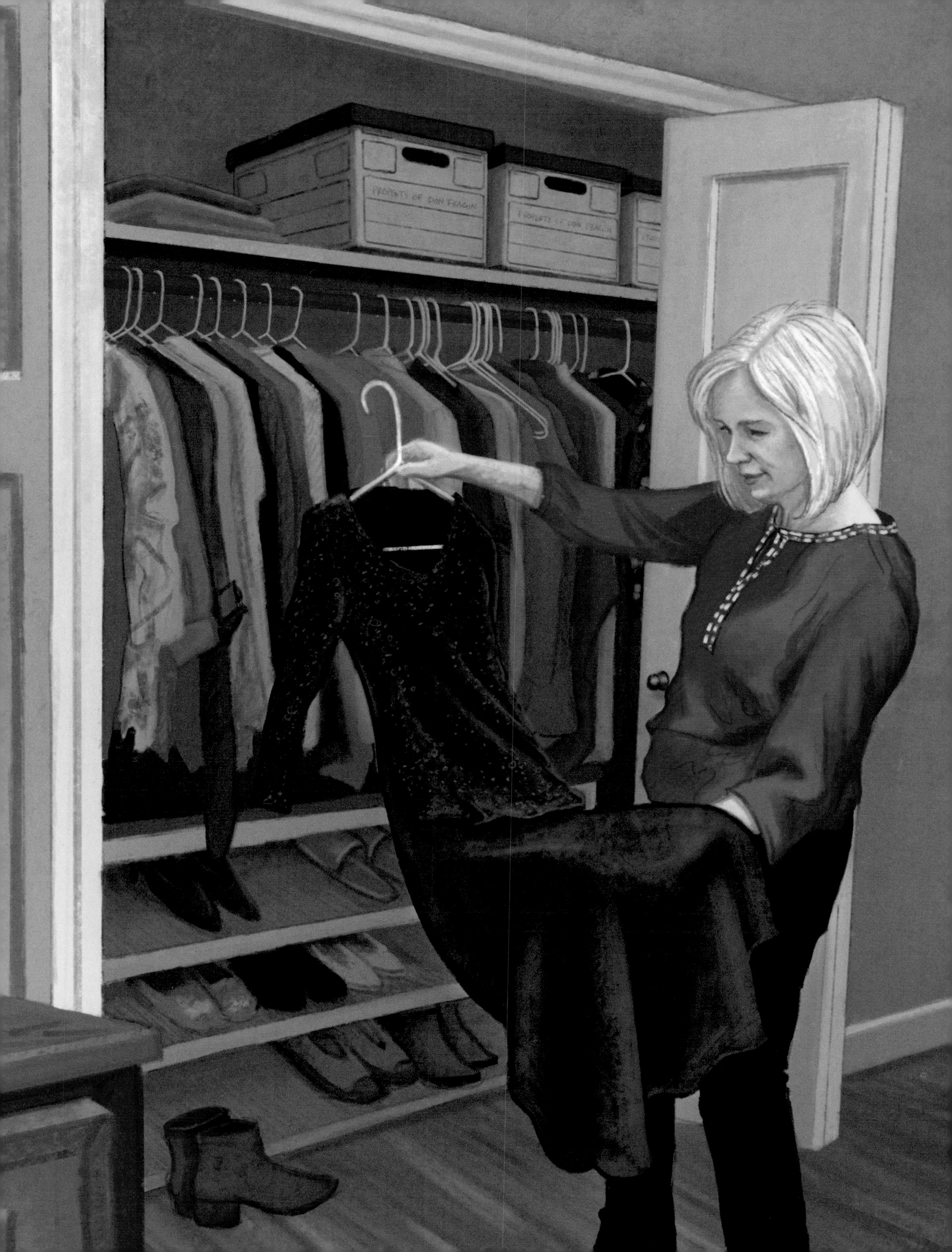
PROPERTY OF DON FEAGIN

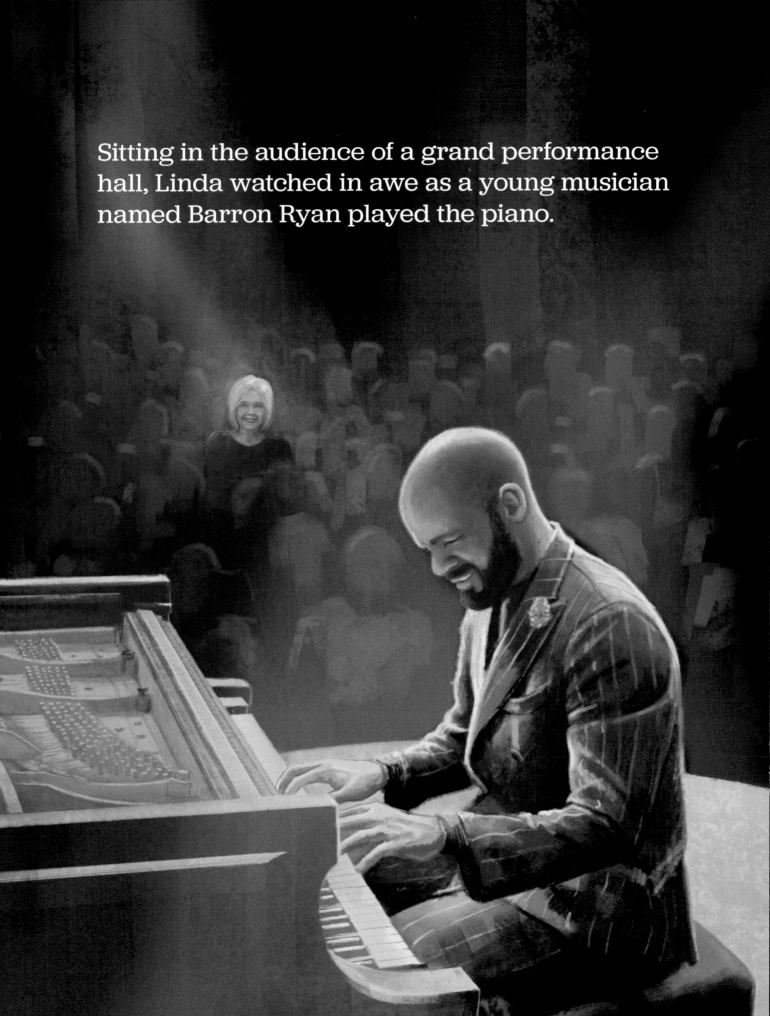

Sitting in the audience of a grand performance hall, Linda watched in awe as a young musician named Barron Ryan played the piano.

His music touched her heart, and she arranged for him to play for a party at her home.

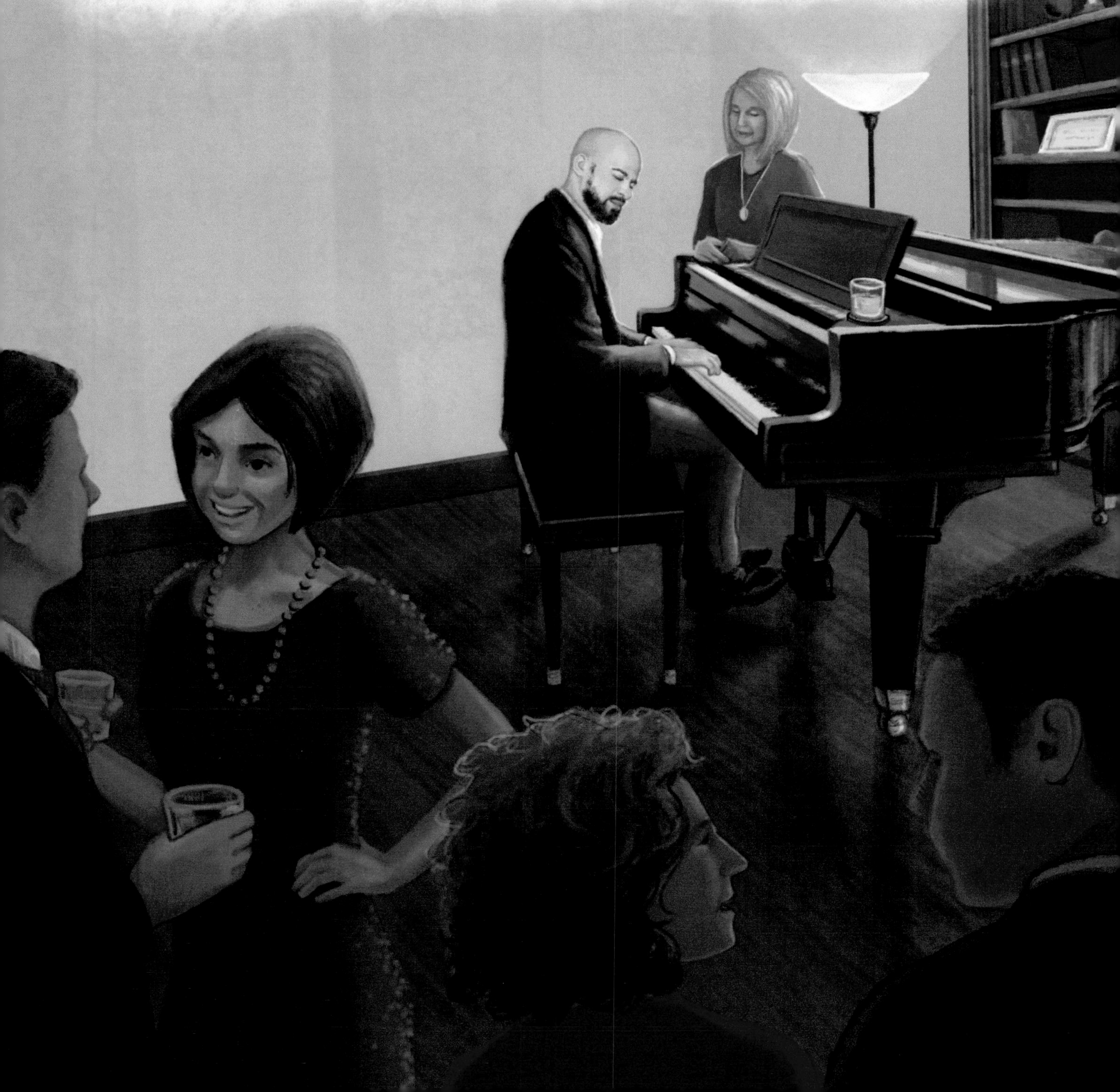

Impressed even more, Linda then arranged for Barron to perform a small concert at her home ...

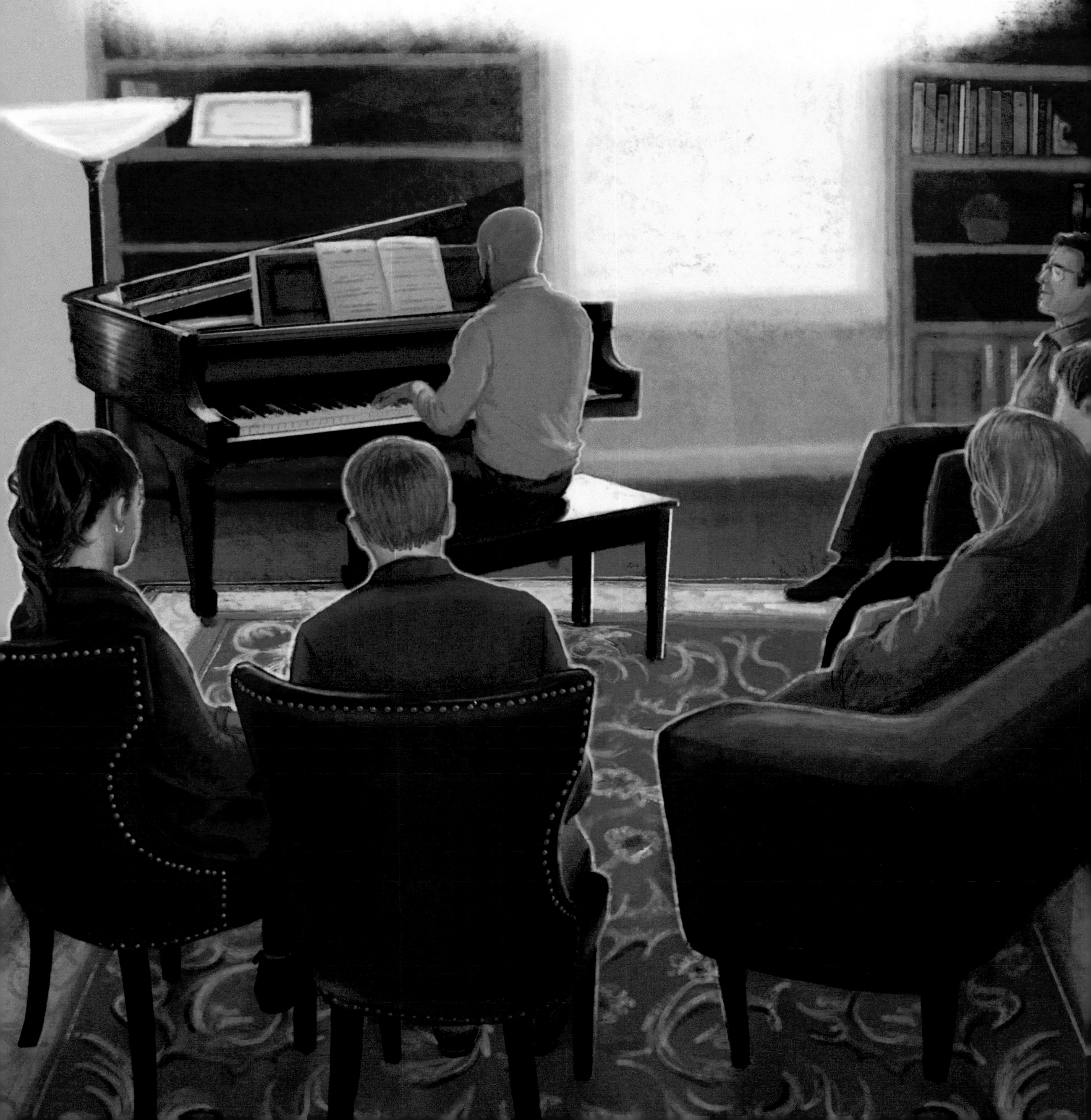

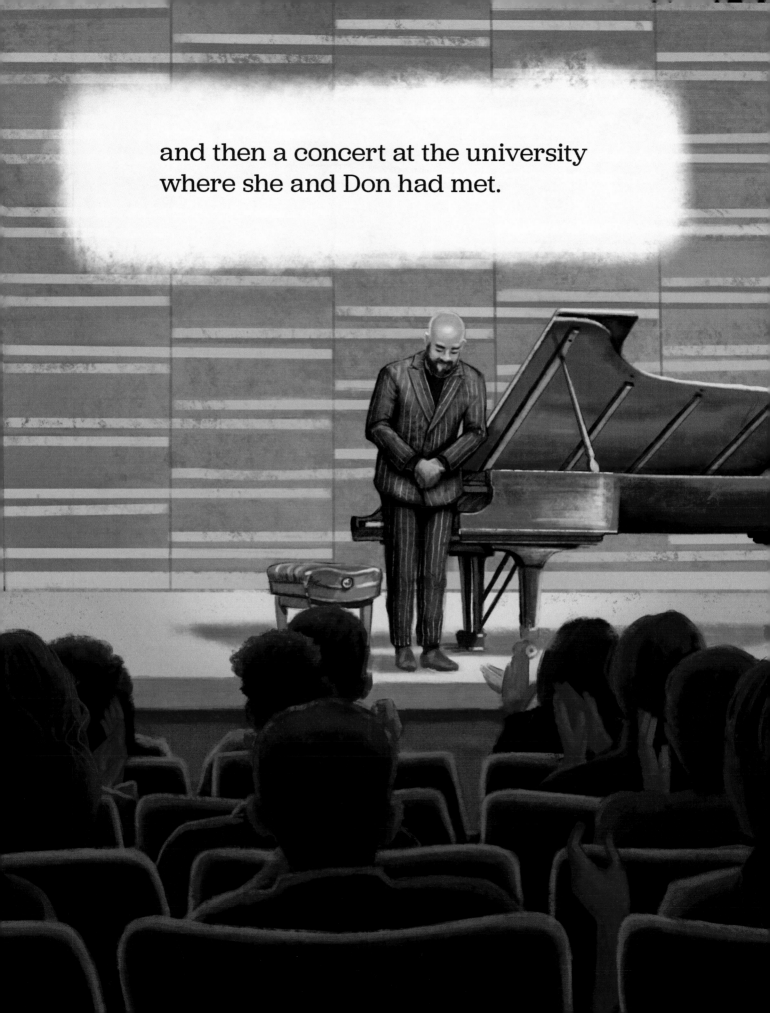

and then a concert at the university where she and Don had met.

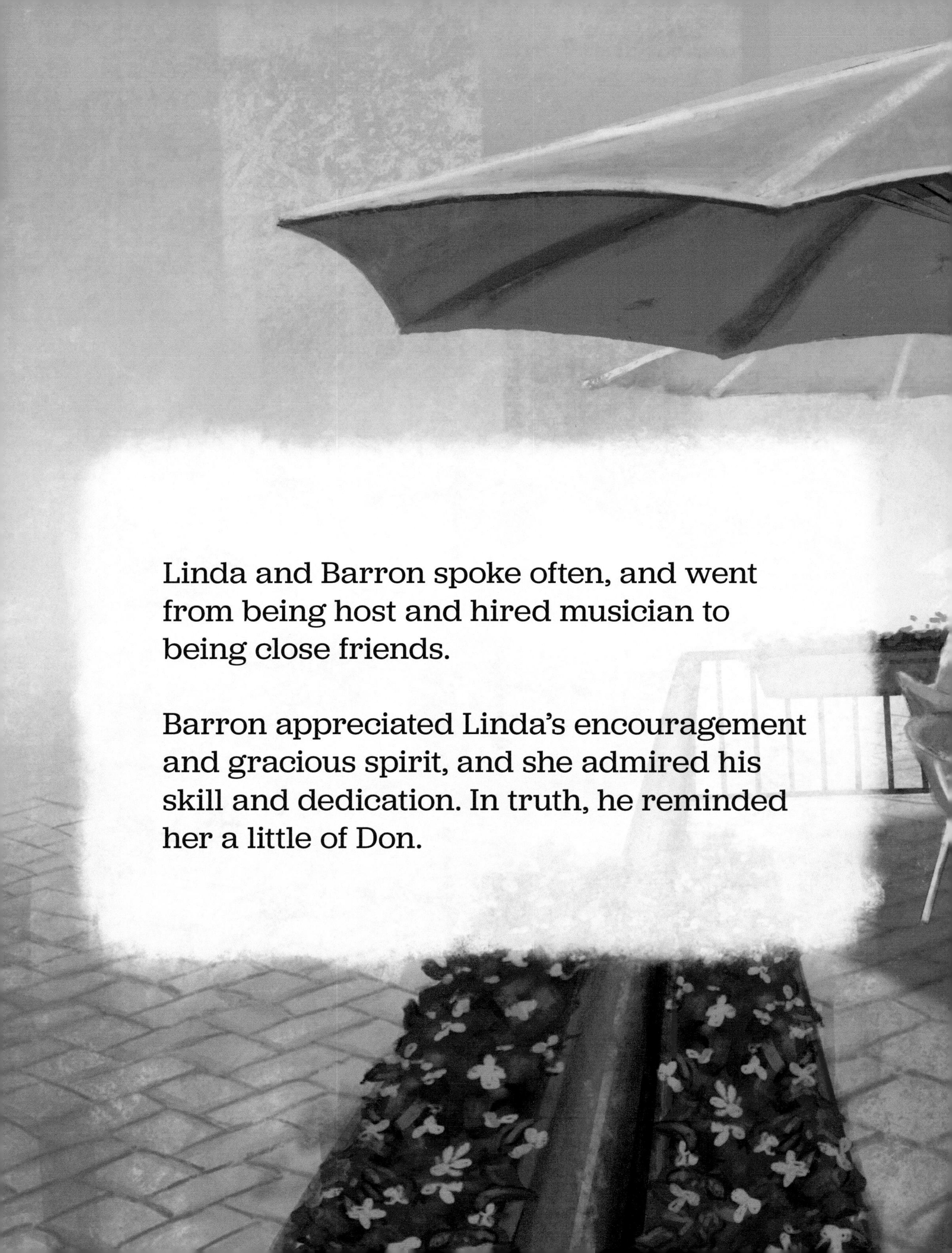

Linda and Barron spoke often, and went from being host and hired musician to being close friends.

Barron appreciated Linda's encouragement and gracious spirit, and she admired his skill and dedication. In truth, he reminded her a little of Don.

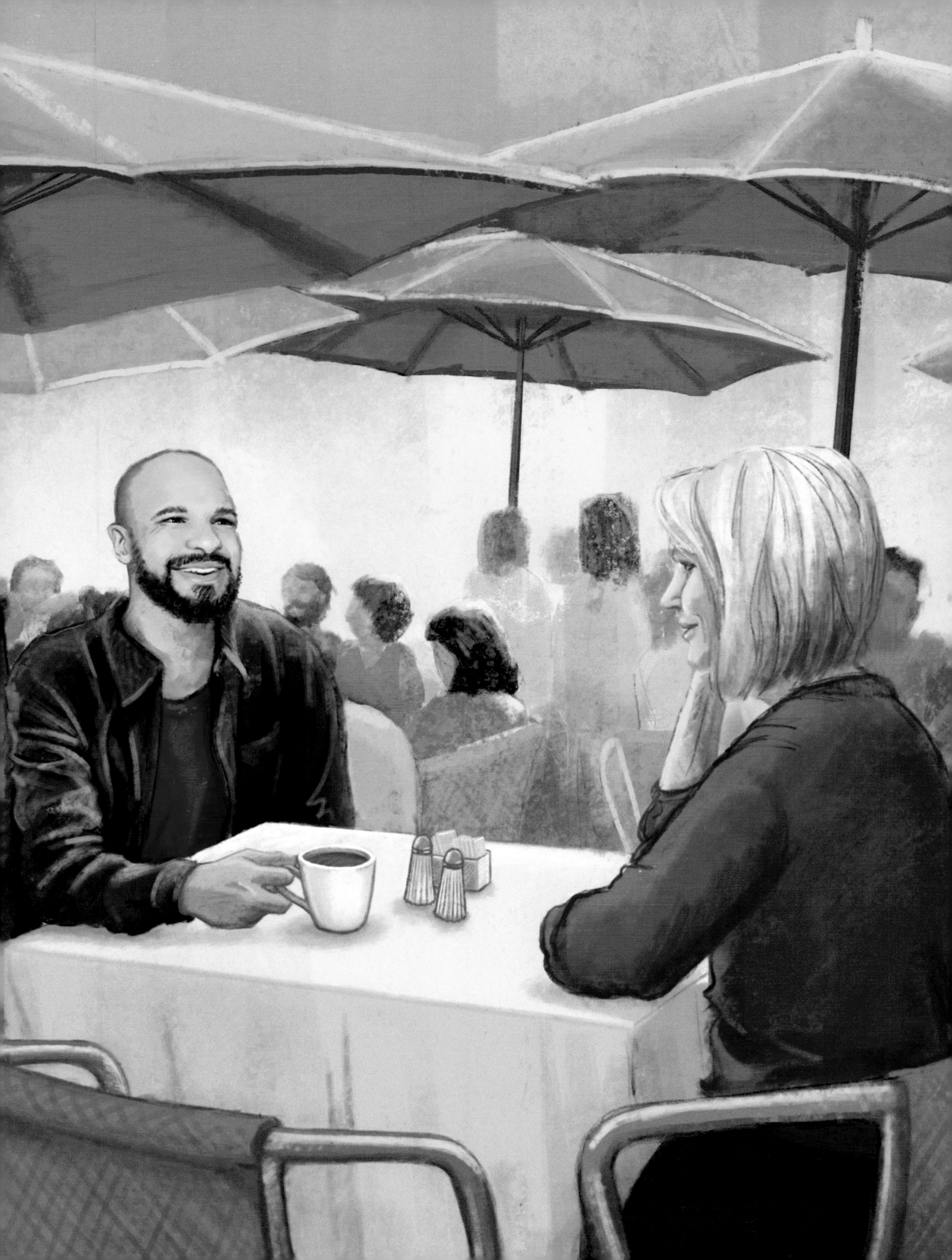

Then an idea struck Linda: what if Don's work could give Barron the inspiration to write new music? So for the first time in forty years, she opened the boxes she'd put away and read Don's lyrics.

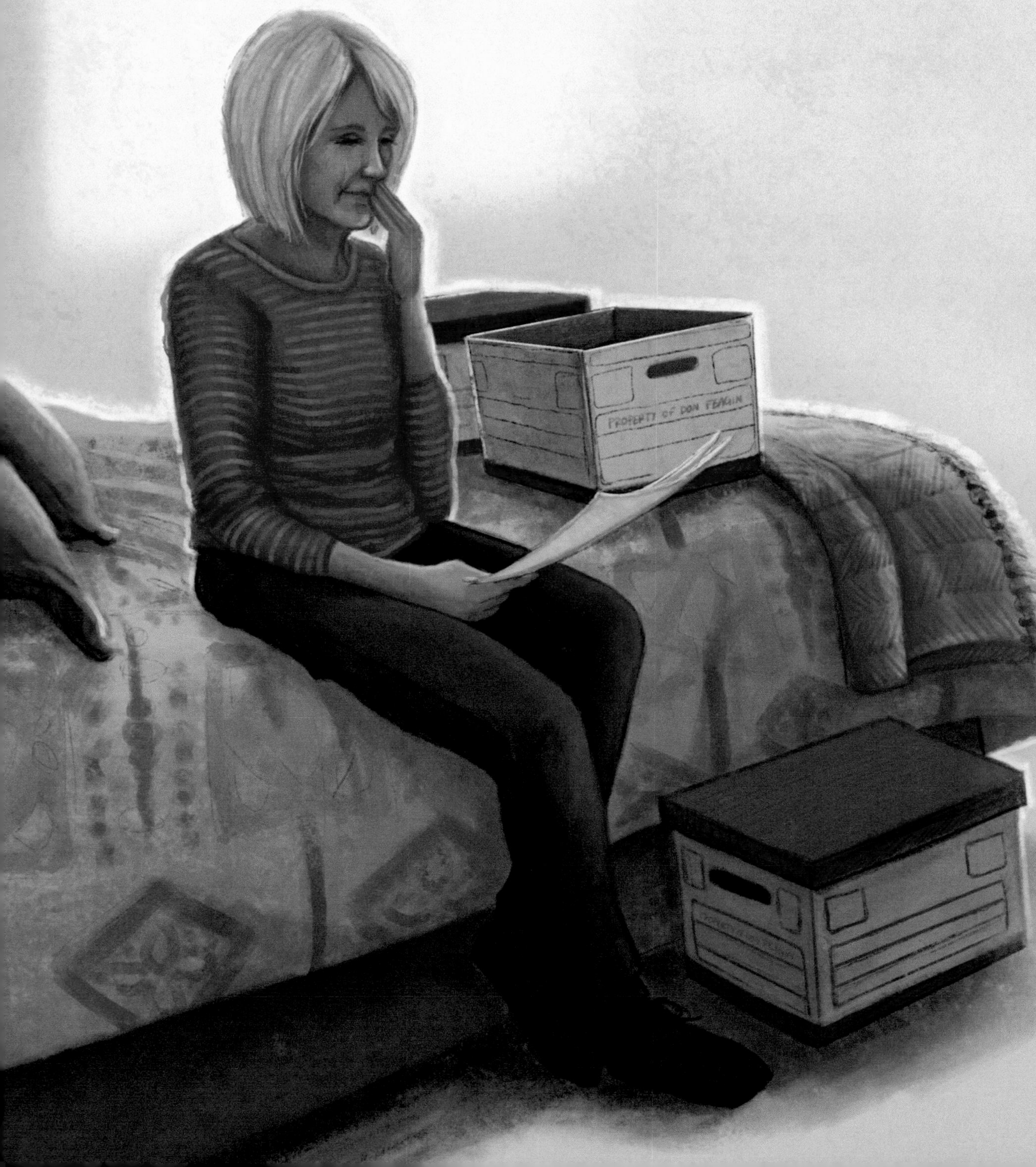

Then she gave them to Barron, not knowing what he would do with them.

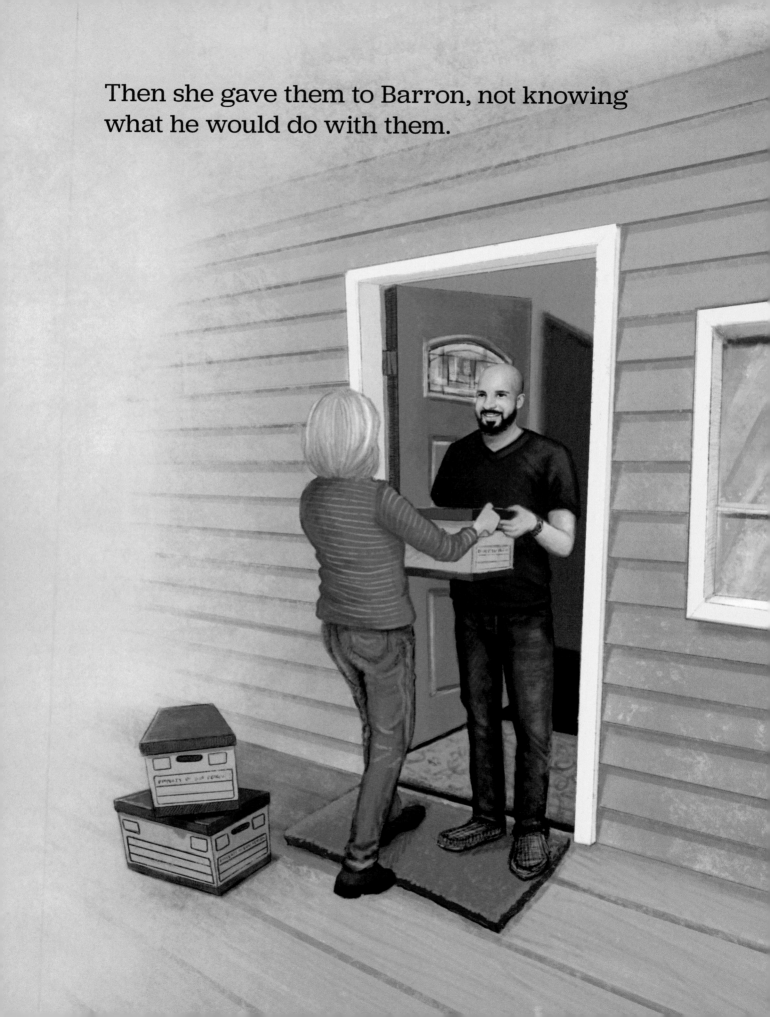

Box by box, paper by paper, Barron dug through Don's work. He found songs about friendship, going fishing, and visiting the local watering hole. But he wasn't looking for those. He was looking for lyrics about Linda.

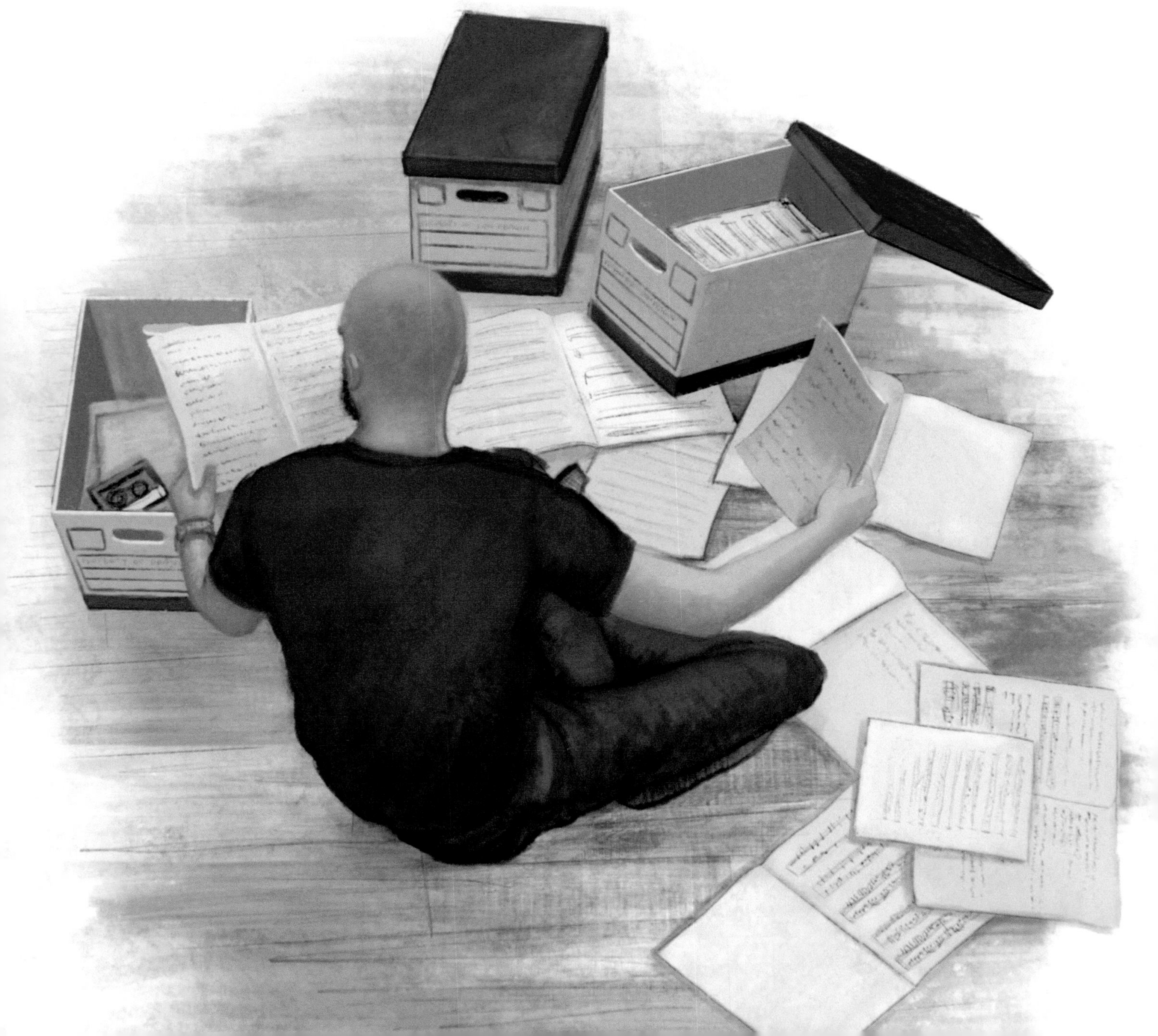

Finally, Barron found those lyrics in a song called "Honey, If It Wasn't For You."

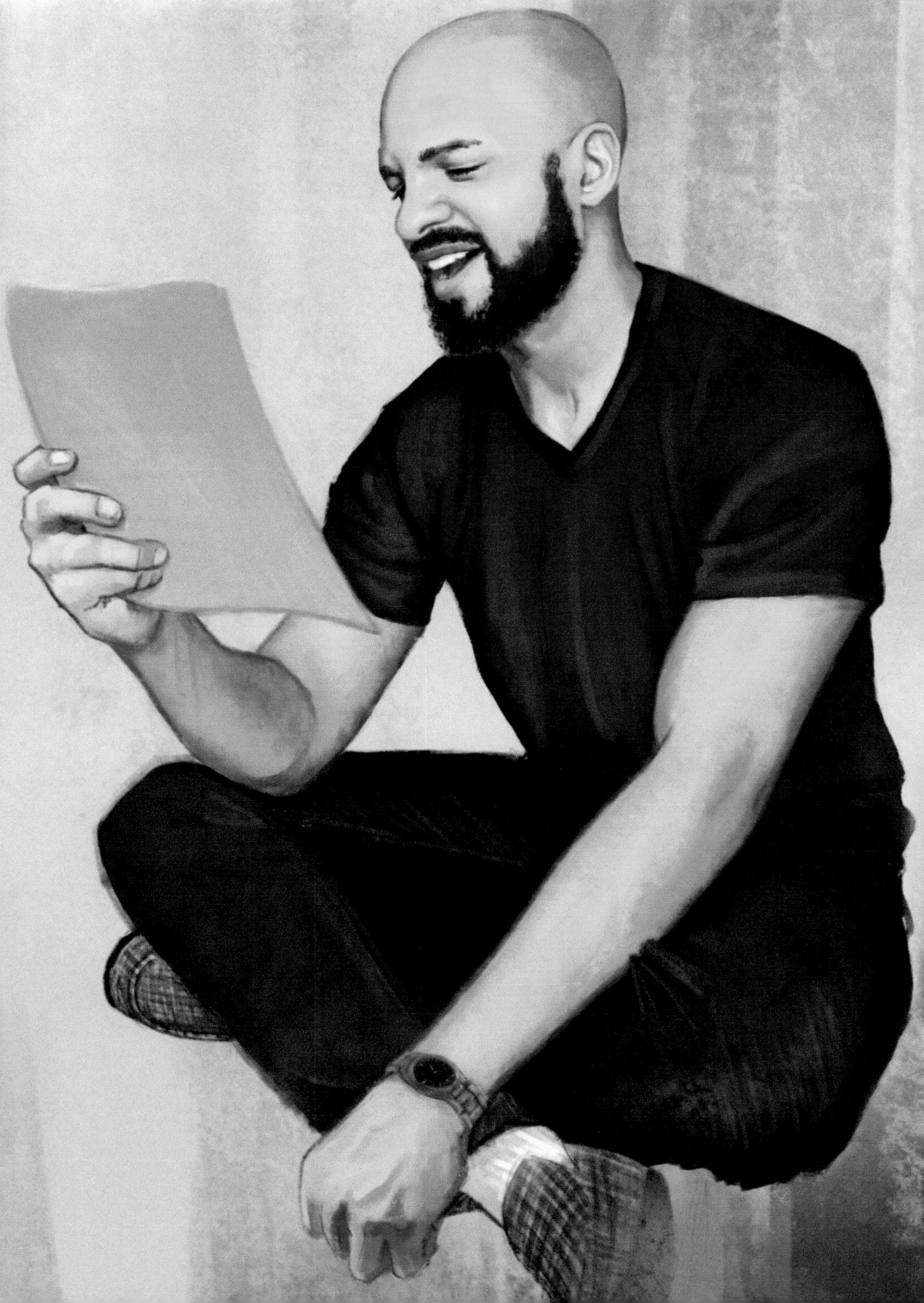

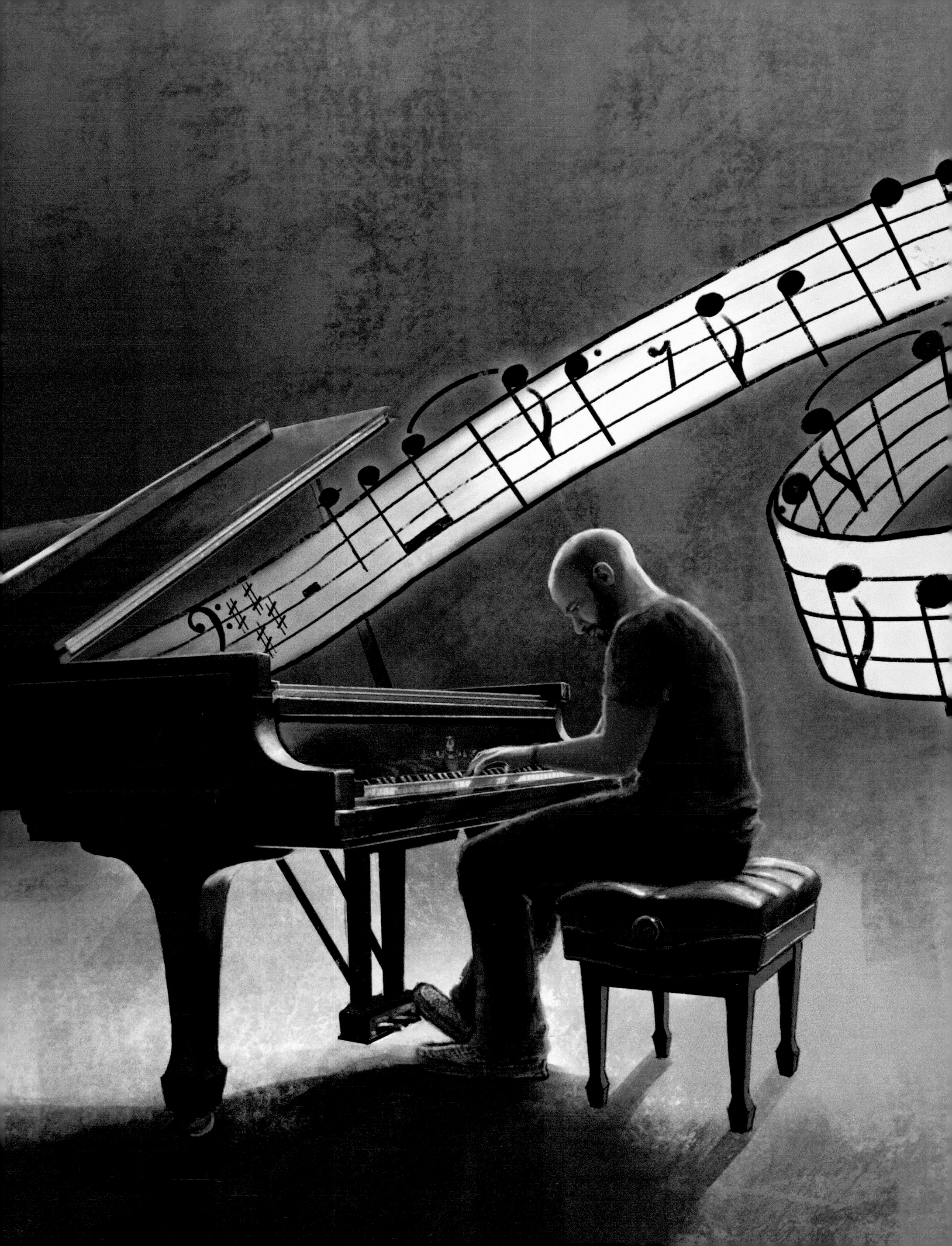

Reading Don's words, a melody immediately jumped into Barron's head. It came so quickly, he couldn't write it down fast enough.

Barron felt exhilarated to set Don's words to music, and honored that Linda would entrust him with this responsibility. He could hardly wait to share Don's and his song with her.

"Honey, If It Wasn't for You" premiered to an audience of one. Barron was excited, but nervous. Linda's was the only opinion of this song that really mattered to him.

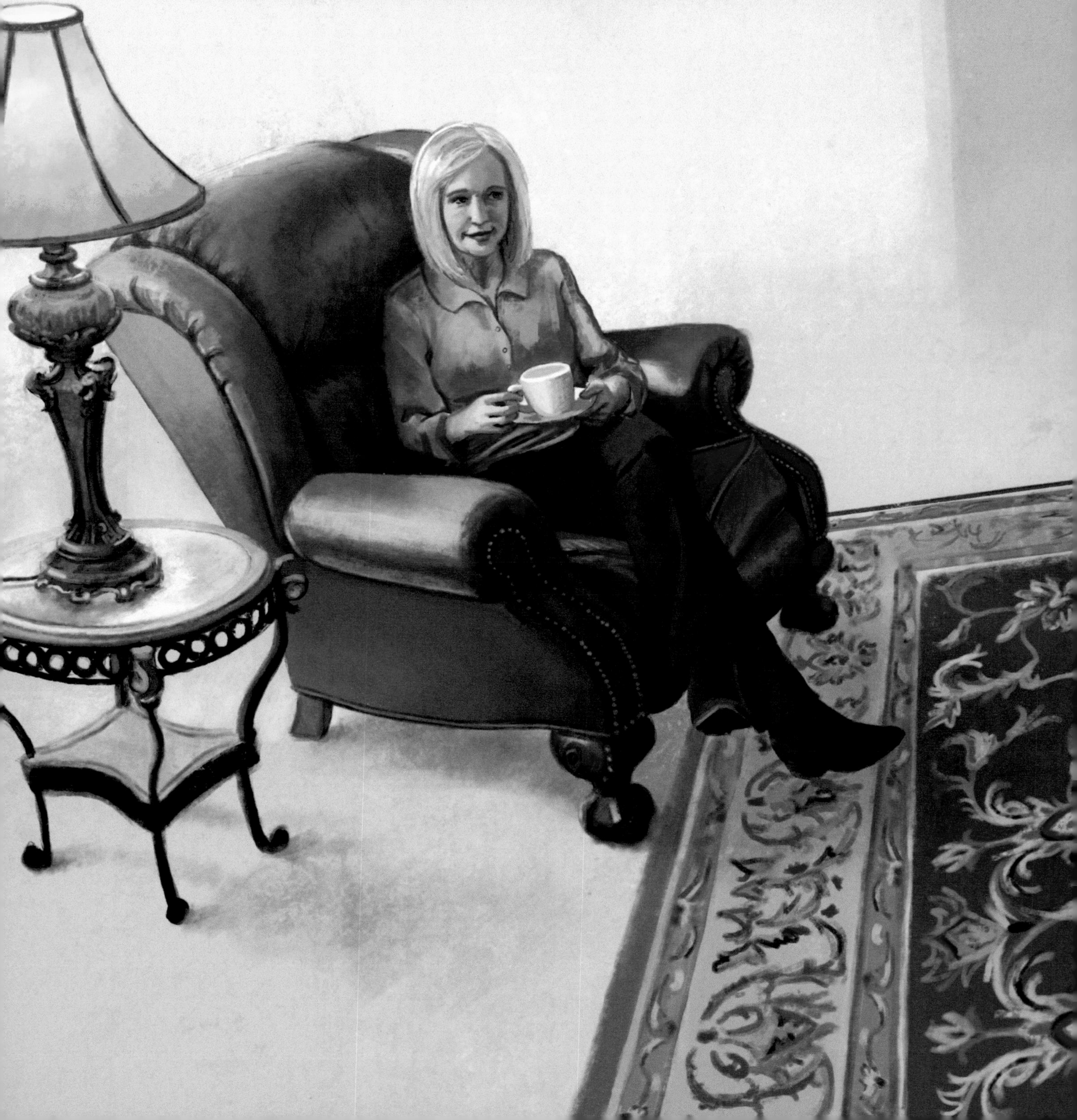

He need not have worried. Linda told Barron that his music brought Don's words to life. It was as if the lyrics and tune had been created together, not separated by a forty-year distance.

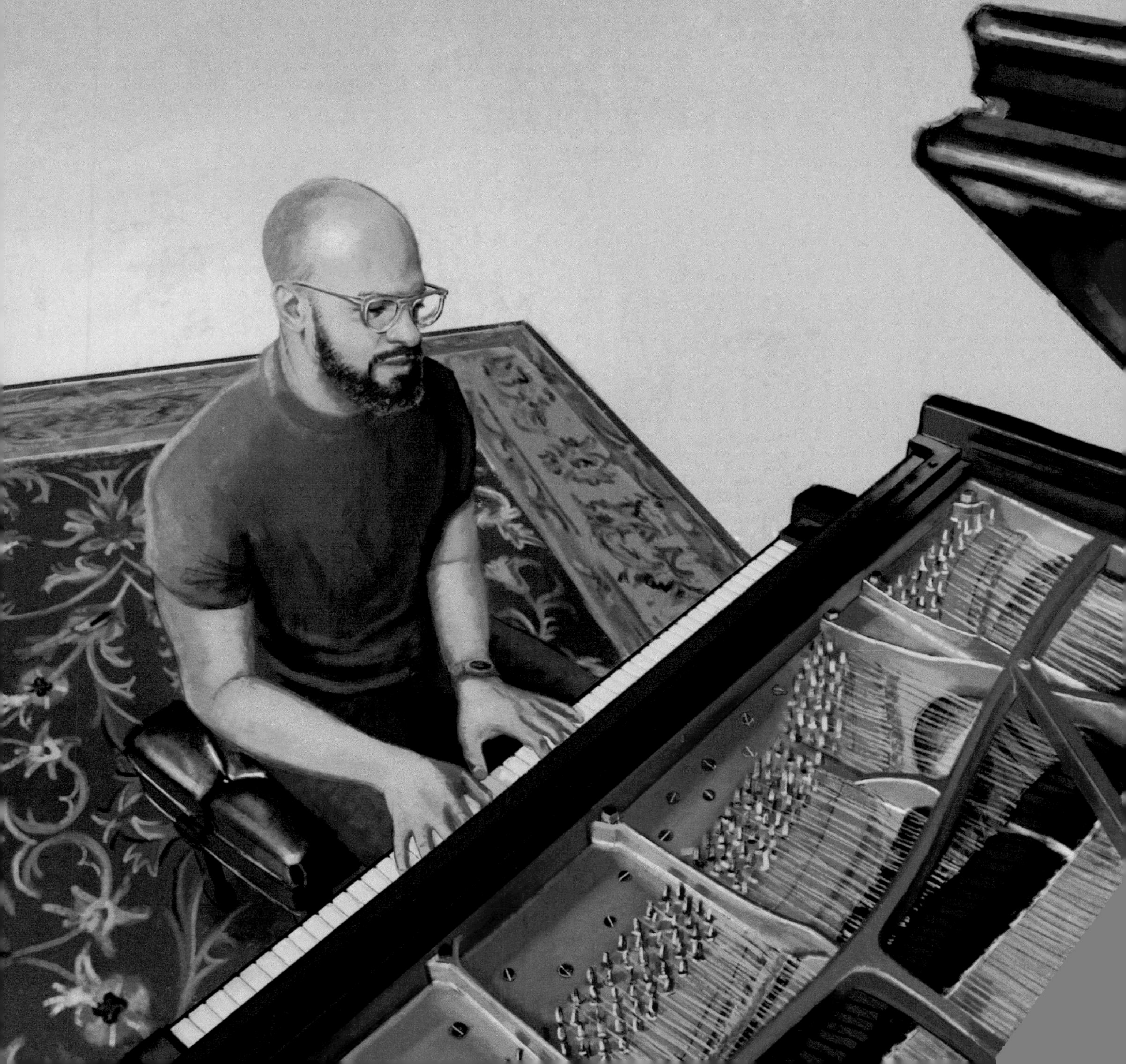

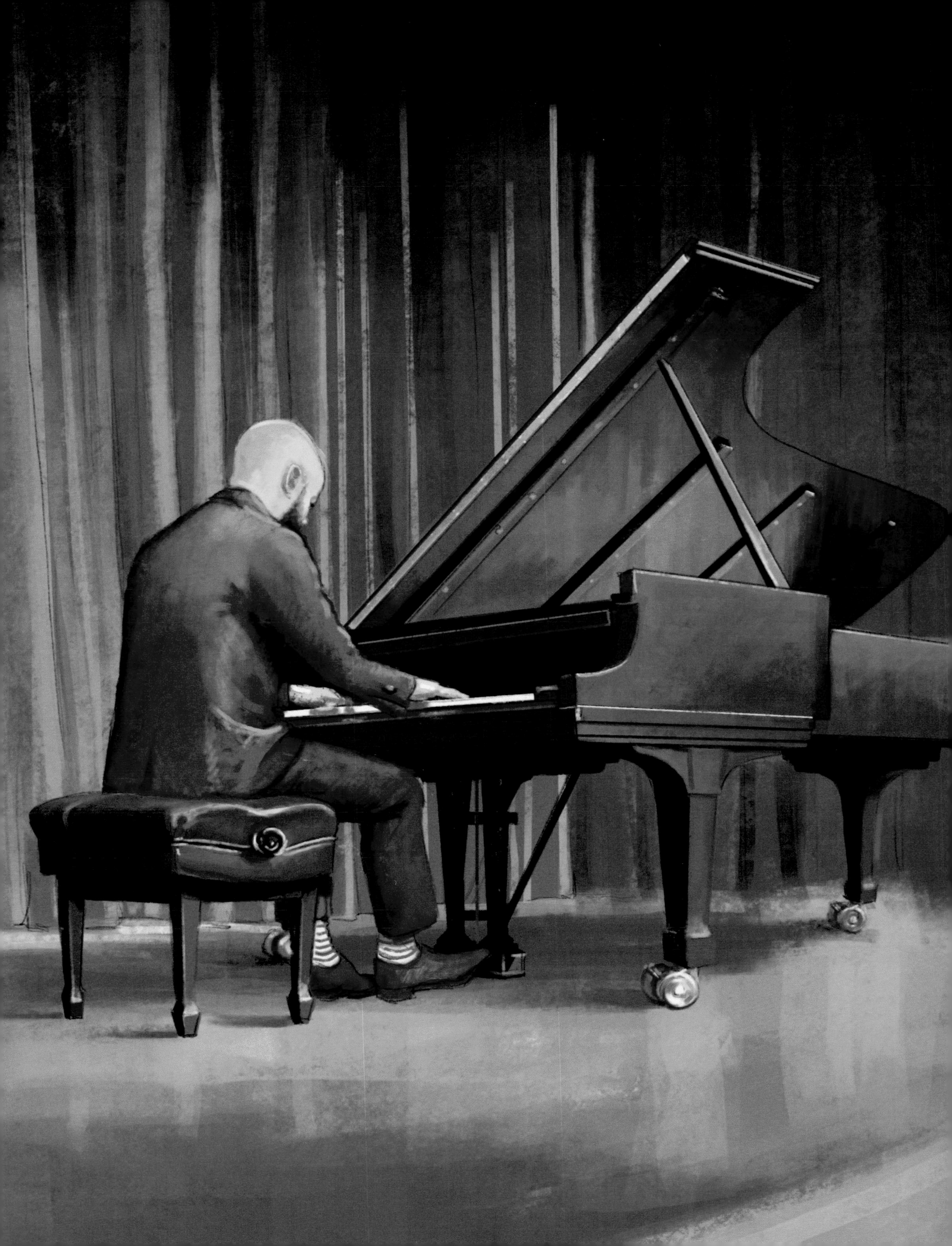

Now you know the story of this special song. It fills me with a sense of gratitude: for love, for friendship, and for all the ways that music fills our souls and enriches our lives.

I hope that you can feel in my melody what I felt in Don's words: the deep love he had for Linda and their life together. That's the heart of "Honey, If It Wasn't for You," and it is that love I hope you will share with everyone who has helped shape you.

**You've read the story.
Now hear the song.**

honey.barronryan.com

HONEY, IF IT WASN'T FOR YOU

Dog

```
        G                    C              G
I was sleeping when she left again this morning
                       C            D
RETURNING TO HER JOB ANOTHER DAY
                C            D
SHE LEAVES ME BACK HOME DREAMIN
            B              C         G
GOT TO  MAKE IT ON MY OWN
         D                            G
I PRAY THE WORDS WILL COME TO ME TODAY
                                                D
SHE TELLS ME HER NEW WORK GIVES SATISFACTION
            C                              D
AND FOR ME NOT TO WORRY  WHILE SHE'S GONE
            C              D
SHE SWEARS IT MAKES HER HAPPY
          B                 C             G
TO LEAVE ME TO MY SPACE
          D
FOR SURELY ITS HARD WORK THAT WRITES A SONG


              G                         D
CHORUS    HONEY IF IT WASN'T FOR YOU
              C                        G
          HONEY IF IT WASN'T FOR YOU
              C          Am  G  F
          THERE WOULD BE NO SONG
              C                  G            C
          HONEY IF IT WASN'T FOR YOU


                                                           C                    G
          NOW I'm PEEKIN THRU THE MORNING NEWS AND LOOKING TO THE TREES
                G                       C                    D
          WHAT MAGIC WILL DIRECT THE WORDS TODAY
                         G
          WHEN EVERY LINES BEEN SAID AND SUNG
                  C                              G
          AND EVERY KEY BEEN TRIED
              D
          THAT SAME OLD SONG KEEPS CALLING ME AWAY


              G                         D
CHORUS    HONEY IF IT WASN'T FOR YOU
              C                        G
          HONEY IF IT WASN'T FOR YOU
              C          Am  G  F
          THERE WOULD BE NO SONG
              C                  C
          HONEY IF IT WASN'T FOR YOU


                G                                    C              G
          AND IF I HAD A THOUSAND YEARS TO WRITE EM' ALL AGAIN
                       C                         D
          THIS IS STILL THE WAY THAT IT WOULD BE
                  C                  D
          FOR YOU STILL HOLD THE TREASURE
                B              C                      G
          TO EACH AND EVERY LINE
                     D
          AND YOUR LOVESONG STILL KEEPS CALLIN OUT TO ME


CHORUS    (REPEAT)              F     G     C
                                C
TAG       HONEY  IF IT WASN'T FOR YOU
```

To Linda Feagin

Edited by Brooke Vitale
Text layout by Jason Yang

Download this book's electronic versions at honey.barronryan.com.

Print version: ISBN 978-1-7365394-2-2
E-book version: ISBN 978-1-7365394-3-9

Charles Patrick Books
1611 S Utica Ave.
Suite 501
Tulsa, OK 74104

Barron Ryan

The son of two musicians, Barron Ryan grew up in a house filled with the sounds of artists ranging from Mozart to Motown. In his own work, he combines those disparate influences into a musical adventure that's vintage yet fresh, historical yet hip, classic yet cool.

Barron seemed destined for a career in music. He began piano lessons at age four with his father, then excelled in performing throughout middle and high schools and as a piano performance major at The University of Oklahoma. But it was only after an international concert tour—the result of winning a piano competition—that Barron found his artistic voice. He discovered the joy of jazz and ragtime-inspired concert music and endeavored to fill the void of funk, pop, and country-inspired classical music. Following his unique muse, Barron has released four albums.

In 2021, Barron wrote a commissioned piece for piano trio entitled *My Soul Is Full of Troubles* to commemorate the 1921 massacre in Tulsa, OK. *Smithsonian Magazine* took note and named him one of Ten Innovators to Watch in 2021.

As was the practice of his favorite composers, Barron publishes his original works in the public domain—offering his work as a gift to the world, and as a chance to collaborate with artists from around the globe. *Honey, If It Wasn't For You* is his first book.

Learn more at **barronryan.com**.

Cali Ward

Cali Ward is an illustrator, fine artist, and teacher with over a decade's worth of experience in the industry. She lives in beautiful southeast Idaho with her husband and four children. Being a mom has brought a new perspective to her art. She hopes to inspire her own children—as well as her students—that they can achieve their artistic dreams.

Learn more at **caliwardart.com**.